Queer Girls in Class

Studies in the
Postmodern Theory of Education

Shirley R. Steinberg
General Editor

Vol. 397

This books is part of the Peter Lang Media and Communication list.
Every volume is peer reviewed and meets
the highest quality standards for content and production.

PETER LANG
New York • Washington, D.C./Baltimore • Bern
Frankfurt • Berlin • Brussels • Vienna • Oxford

Queer Girls in Class

*Lesbian Teachers
and Students Tell Their
Classroom Stories*

Lori Horvitz, Editor

PETER LANG
New York • Washington, D.C./Baltimore • Bern
Frankfurt • Berlin • Brussels • Vienna • Oxford

Library of Congress Cataloging-in-Publication Data

Queer girls in class: lesbian teachers and students
tell their classroom stories / [edited by] Lori Horvitz.
p. cm. — (Counterpoints: studies in the postmodern theory of education; v. 397)
Includes bibliographical references.
1. Homosexuality and education—United States. 2. Lesbian teachers—
United States. 3. Lesbian students—United States. 4. Lesbians—United
States—Social conditions. 5. Gender identity in education—United States.
6. Education—Social aspects—United States. I. Horvitz, Lori.
LC192.6.Q83   371.10086'643—dc22   2010045424
ISBN 978-1-4331-1097-9 (paperback)
ISBN 978-1-4331-1098-6 (hardcover)
ISSN 1058-1634

Bibliographic information published by **Die Deutsche Nationalbibliothek**.
Die Deutsche Nationalbibliothek lists this publication in the "Deutsche
Nationalbibliografie"; detailed bibliographic data is available
on the Internet at http://dnb.d-nb.de/.

FSC

Mixed Sources

Product group from well-managed
forests, controlled sources and
recycled wood or fiber

Cert no. SCS-COC-002464
www.fsc.org
©1996 Forest Stewardship Council

Author Photo by Bj Bowen
Cover design by Helen Robinson
Cover photo by Lori Horvitz

The paper in this book meets the guidelines for permanence and durability
of the Committee on Production Guidelines for Book Longevity
of the Council of Library Resources.

© 2011 Peter Lang Publishing, Inc., New York
29 Broadway, 18th floor, New York, NY 10006
www.peterlang.com

Printed in the United States of America

For my teachers and students.
Thank you.

Contents

❧

ix   Acknowledgements

1   **Introduction**
     Lori Horvitz

5   **Of Quarterbacks And Quarantine**
     Carol Guess

13   **Personal, Political, Pedagogical, Performative, and Praxis: Queer in the Classroom—Five Not-So-Easy Pieces**
     Lee Ann Roripaugh

21   **The Personal as Productive?: Sexual Embodiment and Identity in the Women's Studies Classroom**
     Michelle Spiegel

27   **Dear Diary: A Narrative Journal of My First Years as a 'Fag Teacher'**
     Stacy Fox

31   **Hey Virginia: What's the Writing on the Wall?**
     Jennifer Smith

35   **From Classroom to Family**
       Sassafras Lowrey

39   **The Queerosphere: Musings on Queer Studies and Creative
       Writing Classrooms (On Poetry, Creativity, and the
       Fleetingness of Things)**
       Maureen Seaton

43   **My Battle Armor**
       Liz Matelski

47   **We Weren't Queer Yet**
       Laura M. André

55   **Mr. Short Hair**
       Jessica Gardner

61   **The Week Matthew Shepard Died**
       Bonnie J. Morris

69   **Learning to Be in a Skin**
       Sarah B. Burghauser

75   **"Who Do I Have to Forgive to Move On From This Place?"
       Meditations from a Third World Feminist Lesbian**
       Kristie Soares

83   **Transitions**
       Lori Horvitz

89   **Dr. 'Strange'love Or How I Learned to Stop Worrying and
       Start Loving (in) the Classroom Closet**
       Jules Odendaul-James

97   **Toward a Practice of Humility**
       Mara Hughes

105   **A Teacher's Lesson**
       Lissa Brown

111   **Physical Education**
       Cynthia Tyler

119   **Teaching Out**
       B.J. Epstein

125   **"Imagine My Surprise!" Being Out as a Lesbian Teacher,
       1990-2000**
       Barbara DiBernard

135   **Definition**
       Sandy Woodson

141   **Playing With Gender for College Credit: Experiencing
       Gender, Sex and Sexuality**
       Anne Balay

151   **What My Women's College Taught Me About Being
       Enthusiastically Queer**
       Shannon Weber

157   **Teacher Coming Out to Teachers**
       Mary Clare Powell

161   **Troubling the Coming-Out Discourse: The (Non) Outing of
       My Buzz Cut**
       Anne Stebbins

165   **The Two-Step**
       Holly St. Jean

175   **Contributors**

Acknowledgments

೦

I would like to express my gratitude to my supportive colleagues and administrators at University of North Carolina at Asheville, who have continually encouraged our campus community to grapple with issues of difference and diversity. Special thanks to my colleague, Erica Abrams Locklear, for her guidance in refining my vision for this book, to my friends and family for their support while I worked on this project, and to my students, who always surprise me, in a good way.

Introduction
Lori Horvitz

ℭℌ

At the publicly funded liberal arts college where I teach, I organized a roundtable discussion for a diversity conference, and titled it "Out of the Closet, Or Not: Queer Identities/Queer Narratives in the Classroom." I invited two other professors and two students to speak about their experiences of being queer in the classroom. The two professors, both out and proud, spoke about the general acceptance and support from their students. Afterwards, a male freshman talked about coming out to his friends at school, specifically his buddies on the track team. Although he felt trepidation in doing so, his teammates and friends accepted him. At the end of his short talk, he emphasized how easy the coming out process has been. Granted, the university where I teach is located in a progressive city, known for beautiful mountains, artisans, and a gay-friendly community.

The other student on the panel, a female, never had a problem coming out in literature classes, but once she started taking education classes, she felt pushed back into the closet. When one of her education teachers brought up issues of queer textual representations, her classmates made faces. When it was her time to present a young adult text to the class, she decided to present a queer text, and in doing so, came out as a lesbian. She said the teacher grinned, as if to say, *we have an honest to goodness lesbian in the class!* "After I came out," the student said, "some of women in the class refused to make eye contact with me."

For the remainder of the semester, the student felt like an outcast, a breathing example of the "other." She even heard one student tell another that she didn't want her daughter "to be taught be a dyke." The fact that these biases still run rampant is a testimony to how much work needs to be done, how fear continues to runs rampant, how there is still an assumption that the entire GLBT population are sexual predators.

When it was my turn to speak, I told my story, which started in 1993 at Medgar Evers College in Brooklyn, where I taught my first composition class. I was the white teacher, the privileged outsider to an all Black class. During that semester, I heard narratives of students getting followed in stores, getting stopped by the police for no reason, getting turned down for jobs. By hearing stories, I began to understand racism more so; I also began to confront my own internalized racism as well—deep-seated fears I hadn't been consciously aware of, fears that bombarded me from the media, popular culture, family, politicians, etc.

The next semester, in my composition class I taught *The Normal Heart*, a play by Larry Kramer, a love story that takes place during the rise of the AIDS epidemic in New York City. During class discussion, some students blurted out homophobic remarks: *Why would people choose to be gay? That's not natural! They deserve AIDS! It's a sin*! Now I was the closeted, not-so privileged outsider—feeling helpless, trying to get my students to see the situation from different perspectives. "What if it were you who contracted AIDS?" I asked. One response: "I'd kill myself." I asked another question: "How would you feel if you knew one of your professors were gay?" One female student responded, "I'd feel weird when she looked at me." How could I not feel personally attacked by these comments?

After a few days of racking my brain about how to handle the situation, I tried to gain perspective; I tried to make connections between my experience as the white teacher to an all Black class the semester before, how I was the outsider learning about a populace I was taught, implicitly and explicitly, to fear. But my fears had abated when I listened to my students' stories. In fact, my fear had transformed into empathy. Because of this, I invited a speaker to class—a gay man living with AIDS. He spoke bluntly about his life, joked around, challenged assumptions, turned questions on the class: *Why are you straight?* Afterwards, students thanked me and told me that they understood more so where gay people were coming from. It's clear that when we can interact and connect with someone we fear, when we listen to their stories, we can find compassion for them.

Yet since that time, even in classes where there's a gay-friendly atmosphere, I have never come out, figuring that students in the know, know, and the others don't need to know. But I have questioned myself along the way: do I have an obligation to speak about my personal life, let's say, when issues of sexuality/homophobia come up? Given that I teach at a university with a chancellor who supports a bi-annual Queer Conference, I don't have to worry about losing my job, so why wouldn't I come out? Is it out of fear, or my own internalized homophobia? Why should my students know about me? Shouldn't I have some boundaries?

I'm far from closeted at school; I've taken part in the planning and presenting of work at GLBT conferences and have presented creative pieces at literary readings that speak about queer issues and relationships. Even so, I have remained reluctant to come out to a classroom of students. And unlike other marginalized groups such as differently-abled persons or African Americans, I have the privilege of "passing" into the dominant sexuality, of hiding who I am.

In the early 1990's, every Monday I bought a copy of *OutWeek* magazine from the Gem Spa on St. Mark's Place in Manhattan. In his column, Michealangelo Signoreli railed against then-closeted public figures for what he considered "their complicity in a culture of silence around AIDS and gay rights." When I read his words, I cheered; didn't the idea of someone who chooses to remain in the closet only perpetuate the notion that queers had something to hide, to be ashamed of?

Last year I was forced to confront these questions head-on when a colleague outed me to a class we had been team-teaching. I wasn't in the room at the time, but when my colleague informed me of this, I was angry. "Don't you think that's a choice I should have made?" I asked. Eventually my colleague apologized, but the damage was done. This was the second day of class, a class that was an intensive study abroad program; I lived in the dorms and ate in the cafeteria with students. Some students had come from conservative religious backgrounds. The day before, these students spoke about their discomfort when GLBT issues surfaced in the classroom, how they were taught to look at it as wrong and incompatible with their religious upbringing.

The day after my outing, a female student, after class, asked, "So when did you know you were a lesbian?" I took a deep breath and talked about how my sexuality hasn't always been so clearly defined, how coming out is a process, and how I'm still processing.

Following that day other students confided in me about their sexuality, among other issues. In turn, I felt a sense of liberation. I didn't have to censor myself, lock a part of myself away. Is it that students feel more comfortable revealing personal information when their professor is open? Can the academic learning process be more fluid if there is a general openness in the classroom?

Heterosexual professors don't think twice about mentioning their husbands, wives and boyfriends and girlfriends. So if a queer student sees that his/her queer professor silences him or herself, what kind of model does this set up for students who have their own issues about whether or not to come out? Queer students do need queer role models, and coming out should be a non-issue, but because of the homophobic world we live in, that choice needs to be made by the professor. Despite the fact that my colleague revealed personal information about me, ultimately I had to question why it was such a bad thing if students did know.

Recently a student of mine wrote a paper on how she led two lives, one at the university, and one at home as a "Southern Belle," hiding safely inside what she termed "The Southern Closet." When I asked her why she had to put on an act at home (despite the fact that her parents knew about her queerness), she said, "I don't want to make anyone feel uncomfortable." In response, I said, "Do you hear yourself?" She leaned back in her chair and shook her head. "You're right," she said. "I never thought about how idiotic that sounds."

Might this be the reason I never came out in the classroom? Did I not want to make my students feel uncomfortable? Isn't discomfort where the real learning takes place? As a teacher, isn't it my job to be committed to the process of challenging biases, even at the cost of personal issues and identities? While I write these words, I have to admit that my answer is yes.

After the five panelists spoke at the Diversity Conference, the audience members asked questions, shared experiences and made comments. The energy and enthusiasm in the filled-to-capacity room never subsided, not until the moderator had to end the session to let the next session set up. And it was that energy that inspired me to take on this project, to provide a forum for queer women—both teachers and students—a place where they could address specific concerns, struggles and societal expectations as women in the classroom.

We all have our stories. And when we share our stories, we can collectively listen to and understand each other, feel compassion in our struggles and celebrate in our successes.

Of Quarterbacks and Quarantine
Carol Guess

 confused

A Brief History of Quarantine

The word *quarantine* derives from the Italian word *quaranta*, meaning *forty*, or the number of days land travelers were isolated to prevent the spread of disease in the fourteenth century seaport city of Ragusa. These days, it's useful to draw a distinction between the concept of *quarantine* and the concept of *isolation*. The latter refers to the separation and confinement of those known to carry a contagion; the former refers to the same treatment used on those simply suspected of being contagious (Gensini et al. 257).

I start with the concept of quarantine because isolation has been central to my experience as an out lesbian professor at a small, regional American university. In graduate school, I studied with several lesbian professors; they were out, professionally and socially, but in relying heavily on poststructuralist theory, they de-emphasized specifically lesbian and gay texts. Their courses centered on broad categories like "sexuality and narrative" and "feminism and psychoanalysis." In some instances, their excitement about theory was inspiring. In other instances, they hid behind the texts, avoiding the challenge of acknowledging queer students and changing campus climate.

Acting as if you're post-gay is fine when you went to Berkeley and you're teaching at a research one; acting as if you're post-gay when you've just been hired as the first out lesbian ever to teach at a small Christian college in Nebraska is a good way to get killed. I was gay-bashed and received death threats my first year in a tenure-track position in Nebraska. Yet while I received death threats for being so out, several of my students never realized I was a lesbian. It took years to understand that different geographies require different political strategies, and that each classroom demands a tailored approach.

By the time I arrived at my current job over a decade ago, I was traumatized. I don't use that word lightly: I thought I might die in Nebraska, or that one of my queer students or allies might be murdered. Having moved from a playfully post-gay environment to the terrain of violent homophobia, on my current job I entered a third, equally unfamiliar realm.

I'm grateful to say that many of my colleagues are wonderfully open-minded, progressive intellectuals whose personal and academic accomplishments challenge me to be a better teacher. I count myself lucky to work with these folks. There are staff members and administrators on campus whose integrity I seek to emulate, and whose compassion for students is obvious in everything they do. There are also a few other out queer faculty and staff who are trying very hard to address the campus climate. I don't want to downplay the positive aspects of a job I love, and wouldn't dream of leaving.

Overall, however, the campus climate I've experienced for the past decade is chilly, detached. Visible hatred is rare, but I'm often ostracized from conversations and social events. Ignorance about queer issues is still treated as a healthy norm. In this climate, I've been asked such questions as "Are straight students allowed to take your classes?" and "I don't come out to my students as heterosexual; why do you need to tell your students you're gay?" During a discussion about spousal hires (my department currently has four), I was accused of discriminating against straight people when I observed that this practice is tied to the heterosexual privilege of marriage. At a book signing in the campus bookstore, a colleague picked up my most recent poetry collection, read the back cover copy, and made a cruel homophobic remark to my face. While preparing my tenure file, I was even asked if the jagged edges escaping my otherwise pristine binder were deliberate:

"Did you do that on purpose?"

"No, the department hole punch doesn't work very well."

"I thought perhaps you were making a statement. You know — about being different and all."

Worst of all is a kind of casual shunning, rendering me invisible. Some might call hallway banter unimportant, but hallways are classrooms, too. Faculty meetings, committees, the campus gym, faculty lounges, bathrooms, and parking lots are our classrooms, the spaces where faculty learn invisible, unspoken aspects of professional behavior.

Given the chilly climate, and in spite of my professional accomplishments, it's not always clear to me how I was hired in the first place, but I suspect that my feminine appearance and race privilege were instrumental in declaring me a fit. Would I have been hired if I was a butch dyke or a transman/transwoman who didn't pass? Would I have been hired if I was a person of color? I recall one job candidate, a strong woman who looked awkward in her ill-fitting skirt. She wasn't out as queer, but her gender identity was visible. Discussions about her interview centered on her aggressive answers to our questions, on her lack of warmth, on her awkward demeanor. In the end, she was passed over for a woman with a wedding ring who talked quite a bit about her husband. Another interview, with an Asian-American gay man, went equally badly when several of my colleagues reacted to his slightly feminine demeanor, dismissing him as flamboyant and dramatic. His gender identity and his race disturbed their notions of what a professor should be.

Many of my fellow queer writers labor as sex toy salesclerks, strippers, rent boys, and pornographers. They talk a politics I share and live a politics I don't. I'm privileged, yes, and live outside their center, the urban core at the heart of their texts. I feel stuffy and stern in this setting. Simply having health insurance differentiates me from many of my friends. Yet I feel unkempt at school, where my insistence on the political and experiential aspect of what I study is off-putting to some of my Ivory Tower peers.

I'm in my forties now; like other queers my age or older, I knew I was a lesbian long before I'd ever met another lesbian, or even seen one on TV. Nobody in my world was out; my understanding of the concept of queerness was rooted in blatant homophobia. So vast was the split between my sense of myself as a good person and my understanding of queer people as inherently evil and immoral that I hid what I knew about myself and developed a double life. I lived this way until I was twenty-one. Then I began the long, arduous process of unlearning my own ignorance, and trying to create a life in which my sense of self and my public identity could be reconciled.

Questions and Celebrations

I began teaching at twenty-two. In many ways my professional development as a teacher paralleled my personal development as a lesbian. Stepping into a classroom in my late twenties as a tenure-track professor, I had no idea that this process was unfinished, or that I needed to finish it. I thought of myself as well-adjusted; my teaching and writing careers were successful, although my early relationships were not.

So on my first day of teaching GLBT Studies, I was baffled to find myself unable to speak the words "gay, lesbian, bisexual, and transgender" in front of the class. Stack of syllabi in hand, I criss-crossed the rows of desks, smiling an anxious, fake smile and handing a syllabus to each student. Then I called roll. With seventy-five students, this takes a while. Still we had time on our hands, so I faced them. I needed to talk. I don't remember what I said.

My panic surprised me. I'd been out to everyone in my life for nearly a decade and had published several books on queer topics. It took much of that school year for me to realize the extent to which I'd downplayed aspects of my lesbian identity so as not to offend others. That year, I learned the difference between being out and being visible. In a classroom situation where I needed to speak openly about GLBT issues I froze, feeling shame and stigma I hadn't expected. Yet here was a room full of students expecting me to unravel the origins of that shame and stigma, to move beyond it, to teach them things about queer literature, history, philosophy, and culture.

A significant number of students dropped the class after that first disastrous meeting. Since then, I'm pleased to say that I often over-enroll the class, adding four or five students who beg to take it, claiming it will change their lives. I believe them; it's certainly changed mine.

The context of teaching my first GLBT Studies class amazes me when I think back on it. First and foremost, I was teaching a class I knew nothing about. My qualifications for the class were largely personal; I knew very little about GLBT history or literature beyond my own interests. I'd read tons of poststructuralist theory in graduate school, but the emphasis in my program was narrowly focused on Judith Butler's dismantling of identity. The latter, I soon learned, did not make a good starting point for teaching GLBT Studies at a small university in a suburban town surrounded by conservative farming communities.

Students had signed up for one of the only classes in which we were going to talk about gay people, and here I was saying they didn't exist. I had to learn to set the literature in context—poststructuralist theory, sure, but first capitalism, WWI and WWII, the Civil Rights Movement, second-wave feminism, HIV/AIDS, the War on Terror, and many other factors that shape how Americans today conceptualize sexual identity, sex, and gender. Once I began organizing the class around general paradigms and historical shifts, things got easier. Butler's arguments made sense, instead of nonsense, and students learned that they could pick and choose an intellectual approach to what is, in fact, a hopelessly broad topic.

Looking back, I understand that my expectations for the class were shamefully low. I anticipated all manner of resistance, and envisioned class as a nonstop battle. I thought haters would sign up for the class just to heckle me, and that the few visible queer students would radiate shame.

What happened was in fact the opposite. From day one the class was excited about the material. Most of the students who signed up were genuinely interested, whether because they knew someone queer, were queer themselves, or simply grasped that this topic was central to contemporary American political and cultural history.

One of the unexpected challenges of teaching Queer Studies is that instead of fighting against resistance, I sometimes have to generate it in order for discussion to be productive. As my syllabus states: our aim is to *question*, rather than simply *celebrate*, the identities gay, lesbian, bisexual, and transgender.

Another challenge is breaking down barriers between our class and the university. My students are very good at this; I try to follow their lead. One of my students recently raised hell in a "Women and Literature" class where the instructor refused to allow any lesbian representations whatsoever, claiming they didn't belong on the syllabus. Students have formed groups to push for more gender-neutral bathrooms on campus and for GLBT friendly housing in the dorms. They've started groups like Brown Pride, a group focusing on the specific lives of GLBT people of color, and groups for transgender people and allies.

Perhaps the most unexpected challenge comes from the few students in class who openly identify as queer. They are often my strongest critics, dissatisfied when the course doesn't cover every topic. One year, a number of students identifying as bisexual became increasingly angry with me, with the class, with the world. No representation of bisexuality that I chose for class discussion was good enough; I was biphobic, and that was that. This tends to happen every year, but with a different identity category or event stirring up strong feelings. I listen and learn; I examine my teaching practices and prejudices, but at the end of the day, I also have to let some of it go. I can't be everything to all of them, and they want that, especially the queer students. I do, however, let them know that I'm available to talk, and they crowd my office during office hours.

One teaching method that works especially well for this class is the response essay. Students write five short response essays over the course of the quarter; I grade them pass/fail. The purpose of pass/fail grading is twofold: with seventy-five students in class, five essays each, and a major research paper at the end of the ten week quarter, I'd be overwhelmed if I made copious comments on each response essay. But it's also a great way to find out what students are really thinking. I promise they can write anything they'd like, and I won't pass judgment. I won't fail them based on content, even if that content is angry or disdainful of the material. No question is stupid; no observation is ignorant. The only rules are that the essays must be academic (not personal), and that they must focus on readings and/or class discussions.

In this context, students write honestly about their confusion, fears, and beliefs. I learn who's quiet because they're freaked out and who's quiet because they're shy. I get glimpses of why they're taking the class and what I need to do differently. The essays are often moving; they're also often surprisingly funny. Occasionally a student's essay is a cry for help, and I respond by meeting with them personally, expressing my concern, and directing them to the appropriate services.

As a writer, I use the class as an opportunity to develop new audiences for experimental literature, independent presses, and living writers. A canon of GLBT texts is forming; books like *The Well Of Loneliness* and *Becoming A Man* are examples of texts every scholar should someday read. However, I prefer to bring in texts students might not find on their own. In recent years I've taught Richard Siken's *Crush* and Carl Phillips' *The Rest Of Love*; I often teach Rebecca Brown, Carole Maso, and Eileen Myles rather than Sarah Waters or Jeanette Winterson. For small presses like RedBone Press or Steel Toe Books, an order of 75 texts is a substantial financial boost. My students and I talk about this: not only what we're reading, but who publishes it, and why. Whenever possible, I bring in local queer writers and direct students to readings at our town's fabulous independent bookstore. In this way I connect the class to my other specialty, Creative Writing; in this way I generate new audiences for independent publishing.

Often, the classroom feels like an oasis from the heterosexism and homophobia I experience among my peers. As my students strive to learn what I'm teaching, I strive to achieve the level of comfort they feel with their identities. My bond with them is often deeper than the tenuous or nonexistent bonds I experience with my colleagues.

The Quarterback and the Magnetic Bear

One year several members of our college football team enrolled in my class. Perhaps a homophobic remark prompted coaches to suggest it; perhaps it simply fit their training schedules. Whatever the reason, they were reluctant participants.

Mid-quarter everything changed when a group of openly gay young men decided to infiltrate the football squad's position on the classroom field during small group discussion. Four gay men strolled over to the football players, who'd made a circle with their chairs. Dead silence. Then a cheerful voice: "Let's start on page twelve."

The beauty of the moment was evident to me. Here were young gay men who'd perhaps had a painful relation to institutionalized sports in high school. For once, they had the power. They were smart on this subject, and they had knowledge the football players needed. I don't mean lived experience (although that, too); I mean interest and tenacity. The readings were difficult, but they were prepared. They knew I'd maintain order, and they knew that teasing was out of the question.

I avoided the group, letting them work it out for themselves. By the end of class something had changed. I won't say the football team looked thrilled to be there, but there were a few smiles and inquisitive expressions on the faces of the football players. I stopped by the group to ask how it was going.

"I feel a little weird," said Jeff, one of the football players. "I've never really talked to gay people before."

If there's a secret to my method of teaching this class, the secret lies in making space for the word "weird." Rather than disowning or criticizing students' discomfort with the material, with me, with each other, I make room for it, even when students say things that make me cringe inwardly. The class can't be about mandating approval or demanding that students agree with me, each other, or any given text. For the most part, they come to trust this, and to voice their fears, anxiety, and discomfort openly.

When I teach this course during winter quarter, one assignment centers on Valentine's Day, and the distinction between homophobia and heterosexism. Much Valentine's Day rhetoric isn't homophobic, but it is heterosexist. Conveying to students just how prevalent heterosexist ideologies are can be difficult. Valentine's Day makes it easy, so I send students off campus to find examples of heterosexist rhetoric in town, on TV, etc.

Our class met the day after Valentine's, and I asked everyone to write down the examples they'd found. To my surprise, the first student to raise a hand was Jeff. He explained that he and his girlfriend had visited a store for Valentine's Day. He wanted to buy her something she'd like, and she picked out two little magnetic bears, his and hers.

"Then I remembered the assignment," Jeff said. He wanted to see if same-sex bear couples would stick together magnetically, too. But when he and his girlfriend tried it, the magnets didn't work.

"Magnetic bears are heterosexist!" he said. "It made us mad. So I got her something else for Valentine's Day."

The whole class was quiet. I really wanted to laugh and I really wanted to cry and I felt exceedingly happy.

"That's smart and interesting, Jeff. What a good example," and of course, it was. Then the class jumped to praise him, and I could see on Jeff's face that this experience—of being called smart, of speaking aloud in class, of participating in an intellectual sphere—was new and exciting.

This was what I hadn't understood, hadn't expected: I was not alone on my quarantine island. Although isolated by and from my colleagues, I was quarantined with my students. This bonding, this shared sense of community, surprised and delighted me. It delights me still.

Works Cited

Gensini, Gian Franco, Magdi H. Yacoub, Andrea A. Conti. "The concept of quarantine in history: from plague to SARS." *Journal of Infection* 49 (2004), 257–261.

Personal, Political, Pedagogical, Performative, and Praxis: *Queer in the Classroom— Five Not-So-Easy Pieces*
Lee Ann Roripaugh

෧

1. Personal

I am a hybrid. I grow up bisexual (although I don't exactly know it at the time) and bi-racial (half-Japanese on my mother's side) in Laramie, Wyoming. The first time I get called a dyke is in the fourth grade. I'm holding hands with my best friend, Ruth Ellen Rosenholtz. We're upstairs at the University lab school we both attend, taking advanced placement classes with the ninth-graders, which is why the hand-holding somehow becomes coded as problematically sexual. One of the ninth-grade girls—a pretty, nice one with impossibly flaxen hair who blushes beet red when she gets teased—takes me aside and asks, "You don't want everyone to think you're a lesbian, do you?" I'm not exactly sure what a lesbian even *is* at this juncture, other than it has something to do with the hand-holding. What is, nonetheless, clear to me is that it's not okay to *be* one. I sort of have a crush on this girl, but since I've never had a crush before, I don't know that what I have is a crush. Not to mention that I construct scenarios in my head, in which she's the girlfriend of the pretty and nice boy with long hair who plays guitar. I sort of have a crush on this boy as well, but since I've never had a crush before, I don't know that what I have is a crush. Go figure.

When I come out to my parents—first as bisexual, then as a lesbian, then as bisexual again—my Japanese mother's response has always been denial: "No you not," she says. Then, eventually, she might add:

"Nobody want to know about that kind of thing." Or, "Not until you have tenure!" Eventually, these conversations end with my mother suggesting that my problems with orientation will go away if I go on a diet and lose weight. "First you go on *The Biggest Loser*," she tells me. "Then you go on *The Bachelorette*."

The first time I read a poem containing queer content with my parents in the audience, they leave the reading without saying anything to me, then immediately leave town the next morning without saying goodbye. They were worried, they tell me later when I ask them why they left this way, about running into bad weather.

2A. Political

It is my second year at The University of South Dakota, and I am sitting in as Acting Graduate Coordinator while my colleague and friend, Emily, is on maternity leave. There is a very angry man in my office. He is requesting that I grant him an exception from having to take a course in linguistics. The class fulfills an area requirement. If he doesn't take linguistics in the spring, he will not finish his M.A. degree on time. His objection to taking the class in the spring, he tells me, is that it's taught by my colleague, Susan Wolfe, who is a lesbian—co-editor of the first-ever anthology of lesbian coming out stories, and a lesbian cultural anthology, among other things.

"That's not legitimate grounds for granting an exception to the M.A. degree requirements," I tell the angry man.

"I've never been at a University before where homosexuality is constantly being shoved down my throat," he complains, without even the slightest trace of irony. "Her books are right out there in the cabinet in the department hallway where everyone can see them!"

I resist the temptation to laugh out loud at his unconsciously homoerotic metaphor. It seems clear to me that he's in the midst of some sort of epic homosexual panic. He is also very angry, extremely agitated. I suddenly feel uneasily aware that it's a little after 5:00 p.m., and that most of my colleagues have probably gone home for the day.

"Queer literature and theory have been an established area of academic discourse for quite some time now," I tell him. "It's part of our discipline. And while you're certainly under no obligation to take the linguistics course, I'm not going to allow you to substitute another course that doesn't fulfill the area requirement for it. Your choices are to take the course, or to take a different course in a subsequent semester and graduate at a later date. It's your prerogative."

"I'm going to complain to the chair," he tells me. His posture, tone of voice, are bullying.

"Feel free," I tell him. "But I'm also going to be speaking with him and letting him know that I feel your grounds for being granted an exception are completely inappropriate, and that I don't support them."

"I just feel that I shouldn't be forced to exposed to homosexuality while trying to complete my education," he tells me.

Of course, I'm angry. I want to tell him that Susan, a respected colleague, accomplished teacher, and friend, shouldn't have to be exposed to his homophobia. I want to tell him that he's being exposed to homosexuality right at this very minute and how does he like them apples? I wonder if I should have come out in the graduate poetry seminar, in which he was a student. I wonder if I should come out to him at that very moment. I want to embarrass him, put him in his place, for making assumptions, to feel uncomfortable for insulting me in my office without even realizing it.

"I'm not, under any circumstances, going to grant you an exception to the degree requirements," I tell him firmly. "If you don't like it, take it up with my chair."

Later, I fret. Did I cop out by performing solely within my assigned administrative role? Should I have responded more personally? Should I have taken on a more activist role somehow? Was this in any way a teachable moment? I don't know. I still don't know.

2B. Political

Coming out in South Dakota is still a complex and politically significant act—one that is emotionally and sometimes even physically perilous. Sometimes I can forget this. Vermillion, the tiny, quirky Northern Exposure-esque town in which I live (also known as the "crazy blue dot" in the red state of South Dakota) is a gay-friendly community—one where I can canoodle with a girl on Main Street in broad daylight. Sure, there will be a veritable maelstrom of ensuing gossip, but it will be along the lines of intrusive speculation regarding the goofy train wreck that is my love life, as opposed to the gender of my canoodle-ee. Vermillion is chock full of alternately charming, intriguing, and sometimes irritating, albeit harmless, eccentrics. Apparently a favored stopover between coasts during the anti-war protests of the Vietnam War, the town is full of former hippies, artists, musicians, and, of course, college professors. Women couples openly dance with each other at unlikely venues such as the Eagles Club. During the Vietnam era, the town matriarchs (a couple in which both partners are named Nancy and are therefore known as "the two Nancys"—one a lawyer and the other an artist) held an open house every day at their house on Prospect Street. People came by to gather, discuss peace efforts, and have coffee. The two Nancys continue to open Prospect House to the entire community of Vermillion every New Year's Eve.

Sometimes I forget. Until I'm harassed and threatened by a young man in a truck in Sioux Falls when driving through town with a friend who has a rainbow sticker on her rear window. Until a gay professor at Northern State University in Aberdeen, SD, is shot and killed on campus under mysterious circumstances that, at least according to my queer colleagues who teach there, might have had something to do with his sexual orientation, and resulting in a case whose investigation seems to be inordinately hushed and that seems to disappear inordinately quickly.

Sometimes I forget. Until I realize how many of my queer students— and even a few of my colleagues—are closeted. Until I realize how uncomfortable they may feel about their orientation—many of them coming from small-town rural backgrounds that are politically conservative and deeply religious. Until I realize how uncomfortable they may feel about revealing their orientation to other students—many of whom they've grown up with, and/or who also come from small-town rural backgrounds that are politically conservative and deeply religious. Until I realize how many of them have to make a terrible choice between either having to fully or partially hide their queer identities, or losing their families. Until I realize that the Midwestern ethos of head-tucked-down conformity is not all that dissimilar from the Japanese saying about the nail that sticks up its head getting pounded down. I'm repeatedly taken aback during first-day-of-class ice-breaking sessions by how many students insist that there is not a single unusual/interesting thing to share about themselves during their introductions. "I'm completely *normal*," they repeatedly insist, and I understand that what they're subliminally making a point of saying is that they're—both metaphorically and literally—*straight*.

And in one sense this, I get this. Once again, I'm from Laramie, Wyoming (refer back to *Part 1—Personal*). And so I respect their vulnerability. Their need for privacy and safety. But at the same time, how do I make a safe space within my classroom for my queer students to be out, should they choose to be out? And how do I make a safe space within my classroom in which to challenge students with limited worldviews to broaden their horizons in a way that encourages them—with sensitivity and respect—to question their deeply-held assumptions?

3. Pedagogical

And so I frequently start to create this space by coming out to my students. Coming out in poems I read at local or academic venues. Coming out in my blog, which I know many of them surreptitiously read. Coming out in the classroom—particularly when I'm teaching courses on identity and/or multicultural literature, or when I include queer theory and texts—as a way to specifically frame my own identities within the class discourse. I come out to make a safe space for my queer students to come out, should they choose. I come out to make a safe space for my queer students regardless of whether or not they want to come out. I come out to act as a human shield of sorts, so that the students who consider themselves violently "opposed" to homosexuality feel themselves held accountable to participating in the ongoing discourse with a modicum of respect. I come out because I frequently pass—both in terms of race and orientation—and the coming out causes students to question some of their own assumptions. Even though, in many respects, my sense of identity is, ultimately hybrid, fluid, and liminal, I frequently come out because it is a gesture that, in my South Dakota classrooms, still seems to matter.

Just as frequently, though, I don't come out. Instead, I simply include queer and/or gender theory and texts in my classes as a matter of course. I proceed normally and without fanfare as if the inclusion of these materials is a given—which, for me, of course, it is, but which I also understand, for many of my students, it isn't. In other words, I normalize the fact that I may be radically challenging their belief systems and comfort zones by not making this challenge a challenge. Of course, the inclusion of these materials and discussions inevitably leads to apparent speculation within the classroom, which I sometimes hope is potentially effective. That the defamiliarization of not necessarily being able to fix my subject position raises questions that destabilize some of my students' assumptions. That, for example, my students come to understand that one doesn't necessarily have to be queer in order to be invested in reading and teaching queer texts. Or that queerness can't necessarily be fixed or essentialized in the ways that they might be apt to fix or essentialize queerness.

I am, for different reasons, somewhat uncomfortable with both the essentialist gesture of coming out to my students in the classroom, as well as with the somewhat assimilationist ramifications of not coming out in the classroom.

4. Performative

Queer is not my only identity, and I have absolutely no idea what it means to perform the multiple identities of Asian American, bisexual, Western poet. Most of my friends agree that writer is, perhaps, the identity that I privilege the most, and my writer self resents the literary ghetto created by the terms "Asian American," "bisexual," "Western" poet. But I do feel as if I'm truly a hybrid—with occasionally contradictory elements—and maybe it's this aspect of identity—queer or otherwise—that I perform, both in and out of the classroom.

5A. Praxis

In a bit of a panic, after having been asked at the last minute to fill in on a panel about coming out in the classroom at the UNCA GLBTQ Conference in Asheville, North Carolina, I asked two of my students from my graduate seminar in multicultural literature—students who have since gone on to graduate and become good friends and colleagues—what impact, if any, my coming out in the class had for them at that time. I was curious, and I also hoped that I could use their comments to fill in what I was scared might turn into fifteen minutes or so of either dead air or hot air. Here's what they wrote to me:

Annie Christain:
Personally, the fact that you came out in the classroom struck me as a very bold and brave thing to do. I came out to my mom and some friends as an undergrad, but since I moved to a new state for graduate school, I needed to come out again. I didn't do this until well after I took your class, but even

though I needed more time to be comfortable enough with myself to make this move, you definitely gave me the hope and encouragement that I could do the same.

I also think that one can never know how something like a professor coming out in classroom can affect students, especially in South Dakota. Vermillion is gay-friendly, but this is not true in other parts of South Dakota and northern Iowa. If students from those areas are used to feeling ashamed about their orientation, if a professor comes out, that could automatically give them an ally and the confidence to come out as well. I thought I was the only lesbian in the class, but it turned out that someone else who took the class is as well. In a sense, you gave us a voice, while also forcing students who aren't gay (or who may be in denial) to discuss, think, and write about themes and issues that open up the range of possibilities for human and literary expression.

Lindy Obach:

I went home and told my girlfriend, "I think Lee Roripaugh came out in class tonight." And that blew my mind. I came to USD from an undergrad town full of conservatives and military personnel and before that, a farm in Southwest North Dakota where no openly gay people exist. All through growing up, I attended Catholic mass and wore ribbons on my letterman's jacket to show my disgust at things like abortion and pornography. "Faggot" and "dyke" were words thrown around all the time. People were not gay. You just simply were not gay. It wasn't even a possibility.

I slowly came out to Lee and the other writers in our poetry workshop class that semester, but not verbally. I never told anyone I had a girlfriend, but my poetry discussed themes of strict gender roles, lesbianism, and identity. In the poems that only Lee gave feedback to, I was more explicit and wrote things about two women being together. Now that I knew Lee a bit better and had found her blog, I grew more comfortable around her. Without saying it, I wanted her to know I was like her. Keep in mind, I had only ever met one other woman in my life that wasn't straight, and I am pretty sure she was just experimenting.

In the three years that I have been a teacher, I have told my brother, my sister (for now, the thought of telling my parents still causes me to black out), my closest high school friends, my closest college friends, my wonderful friends in Vermillion, the whole town of Vermillion, and probably most of USD that I am a lesbian. I am finally being verbal. While I do not announce my lesbianism in the classroom, I consistently bring up current gay issues with my students. We talk about gay marriage, gay adoption, Amendment C in South Dakota, Proposition 8 in California, hate crimes, etc., etc. I approach my courses as cultural studies, and have been inspired by my students. For the most part they are, perhaps surprisingly and always touchingly, aware and sympathetic to the plight of gay Americans. I have pictures up in my office of my partner and I and I bring her to relevant departmental events. My lesbianism is not even a "thing" anymore. It just is.

5B: Praxis (A Post-Script of Sorts)

It is my second semester at USD, and I've started seeing a woman and we are constantly seen around town together, canoodling and whatnot on Main Street. A strange thing happens in my Intro to Creative Writing class. An inordinate preponderance of the fiction projects turn up with a surprise/twist ending of the OMG! She's a lesbian! variety.

I realize that it's a small town, and that people know things about me, but I'm not used to it. It's unnerving to be naked in the locker room at the gym and have someone come up to me and tell me: "You're the new poet, aren't you? You're renting that little yellow house on Elm, right? Did you know your yard is full of snakes?"

I realize that if I've been canoodling with a girl on Main Street, it's the FaceBook equivalent of posting a status update to the entire town that reads, "Lee Ann Roripaugh has been canoodling with a girl on Main Street." I realize that "Lee Ann Roripaugh has been canoodling with a girl on Main Street" might as well be in a scrolling neon marquee on the Jones Supermarket sign everyone drives by several times every day on Cherry Street, Vermillion's other main drag.

I realize my creative writing students have probably been hearing things, and I'm unnerved by what feels like an unauthorized movement from teacher to subject to object. I'm still not entirely sure what to make of this. But then I think of Cathy Griggers' "Lesbian Bodies in the Age of Postmechanical Reproduction," and I wonder if not only have I been queer IN the classroom, maybe I might also be, at least a little bit, queerING the classroom.

The Personal as Productive?
Sexual Embodiment and Identity in the Women's Studies Classroom
Michelle Spiegel

છે

In my educational career prior to college, I wasn't exposed to even one queer-identified, "out" educator. I fully believe that this contributed to my denial of being queer—there were no role models, no people in my life to show me that there was something other than being heterosexual, and furthermore, that that was okay. And so throughout my elementary, middle and high school years, as I look back on those times, I recognize that I dismissed any possibility that I could be a lesbian, and consequently hyper-feminized and hyper-(hetero) sexualized myself as proof to others and to myself that I was in fact straight. The only experience I had of a queer educator during that time is now a recollection of rumors circulating the school of a "dyke" gym teacher who we speculated would stare at us while we changed in the locker room. Fortunately, my luck changed as I went on to my undergraduate career and began taking classes in the Women's Studies Department. Not only was I finding the material enthralling, but I had numerous professors who were queer and more than willing to discuss what that meant to them as individuals and how their sexual identities were fluid, temporal, conditional, and continuously shifting. Their candidness with their class encouraged us as students to be candid with them, to respect them and feel like we wanted to share as well; this made the class open, made us want to challenge each other and even the professor, and to start questioning our own positionalities and identities in society.

Although I was enjoying my newfound critical consciousness and freedom in my Women's Studies classes, as an Elementary Education major, I was still haunted by the idea that all teachers were and had to be heterosexual and normative. This idea was confirmed for me when I participated in my practicum teaching. Two particular memories stand out to me. The first was my experience in the faculty lounge during lunch when all of the teachers were discussing what they did some particular weekend with their husbands and children and blatantly asked my colleagues and me about our boyfriends. I remember being stunned, frozen—I didn't know how to respond and so I didn't. Their (perhaps unknowing and subconscious) heterosexism had silenced me. I decided in that moment to censor myself rather than be made an obvious outsider. Another moment occurred when the teacher I was observing made a snide side-comment to me about two of the first grade boys who were holding hands in the choo-choo train on the way to recess; she then quickly addressed the situation by spectaclizing them and telling them that boys don't hold hands, while she switched around the children so that the order was boy-girl-boy-girl. Again, another moment in which I should have said something, because now at the early age of six, this entire class got a lesson on gender and sexual normativity. These experiences are part of the major reason why I ultimately decided not to go into Elementary Education (despite the fact that I love children and have a passion for teaching) and never finished that degree. Yet I now recognize the immense power that teachers can have in disrupting these heteronormative spaces, strategies that can be deployed, and the fact that there are ways in which I could have fought to feel accepted in that community. I wish more than anything that I could have returned to those moments and stood up to the teacher, to have been part of dismantling the heterosexist structure of the educational system.

Now, as a twenty-three year old graduate student and a teaching associate, responsible for teaching undergraduate students in a Women's Studies classroom, I'd like to think that I still do that sort of work but in a much different context and in a much different way. I decided I was going to "out" myself on a whim my first quarter teaching. We were doing an activity on privilege and one of my self-identified heterosexual students couldn't understand how she had any sort of privilege over homosexual people besides the right to marry. I quickly jumped in, almost defensively, and gave a laundry list of things that were heterosexist in our society, in institutions such as law, the school, religion, the media, etc. that I experience because I'm a lesbian. That particular student, along with a few others just stared at me with jaws agape. I asked why they were looking at me like that and they responded that they had no idea that I was gay. In that moment it was really productive for some students in my class because my "passing" body (which does not appear stereotypically "butch") had been (homo) sexualized, disrupting the heterosexist space of our classroom created by the previously contended statements, and had the potential to make those students think twice before making such comments in the future; yet it was also not the right way to come out. I never again addressed my sexuality with that class except to mention that I was going home to make my partner dinner, and although I pushed our conversations to continually address GLBTQ issues, one of my students wrote on my evaluation that she felt like if she wasn't a lesbian she couldn't survive in my class. This was clearly not the way I wanted my coming out to affect my students!

Many teachers have been taught, both explicitly and implicitly by administration, parents, students, fellow colleagues, media/popular culture and even at times and in some states—the law—that there must be and remain a separation between their (public) identities as educators and any other (private) identities. We occupy this unique, dualistic space of being both void of sexuality and providing necessary surveillance of students' sexual bodies and yet outside of school, we're expected (ironically) to be quite sexual—but normatively so—heterosexual, married, and with children. That is, in school, teachers are not expected to exist in the social world with private lives unless of course, they're mentioning how they're picking up their children from soccer practice or displaying a picture of their husband on their desk. This cultural prescription begs the question: Are queer teachers' only alternatives to be single and asexual or in hiding, maintaining rigid boundaries between our sexual lives and identities?

I believe that a lot of what informs this need for dualism is how we have historically constructed and romanticized the child (and childhood more generally) as innocent, pure and needing to be "protected" from certain information—particularly about sex, sexuality and even more specifically that which is non-normative. We cannot deny and divest youth of their sexualities, their sexual desire and agency, and more importantly that they bring all of that into the classroom. This also affects how we have conceptualized the classroom, as based in a mind/body split. We need to rework the idea of the mind/body split where the body is a complete and separate, contained entity which has no space in the classroom. We need to complicate the idea of the classroom as solely a place for "intellectual" work and acknowledge the fact that many times, intellectual work requires and benefits from an understanding and incorporation of the personal (as all students bring different experiences and backgrounds to the classroom that help to inform their lenses/ways of viewing/knowing the world and understanding course material). And we cannot deny the fact that all teachers of all grade levels teach a great deal about sex whether intentionally or not!

After that first quarter of teaching and my failure to come out in a productive way, I vowed to work to make my classroom a space where students could interrogate both (sexual) identity and the social world in which they live. And in order to do that, I needed to challenge not only the aforementioned, but also this idea, which is so prominent in Women's Studies classrooms, of the "safe space." First and foremost, I ask of this space—safe for whom? What "kinds" of people feel safe to disclose personal information, to grapple with course material and other students, to be able to be fully present and reap the most out of their educational experience? Within a dominant understanding of safe space, the answer to this question is the students and teacher(s) who are normative and gender/sexuality conforming. Discomfort will inevitably arise in a classroom where course content works to disrupt and complicate students' prior understandings (dominant assumptions) of themselves and this social world in which they live. My hope is that the course I teach encourages students to reflect honestly and tirelessly on their own sexualities and how they came to understand, realize and define them (and under whose **mis**guidance). I (and many others) believe that this idea of a safe space is not productive and that it in fact, might be counterproductive. We need to trouble the idea of a true, essential self, underpinning the notions of "navigation" and "being yourself" within this safe space. Although I of course want my students to be able to come forth and speak about personal and past experiences in a way that they do not feel they will be attacked or judged by me or their colleagues, I encourage critical inquiry which, because of the nature of the deconstructive work it entails, sometimes requires that discomfort and threat be present in order for transformation to take place. Ideas about sexuality need to be discussed openly and sometimes uncomfortably in order to fully expose the inner-workings of how we have come to know about it in order to change it, society and ourselves.

My goal, again, is to create a space in which students obviously feel "safe" enough to share, but are also asked, encouraged, and want to challenge their preconceived notions of each other, and me, in order to create joint knowledge based on both past and current experiences and understandings.

I believe that my sexual disclosure encourages this kind of critical work. That I am able to be honest with my students, often allows for honesty in return. While some educators experience the pain and internal anxieties about censoring their sexual identities, which undoubtedly affects their pedagogy and practice, or suffer negative consequences such as harassment, job dismissal, and/or gossip once breaking the silence, I feel that I am lucky enough to not have had to face those difficulties. My coming out serves for me as a form of liberation, a form of political and personal empowerment—a moment of agency. And simultaneously I am careful that I do not alienate those students who are heterosexual and believe I may have biases. I am careful that I am not coming out in order to make my students tolerant in the neoliberal sense of "valuing" diversity only when I'm a certain kind of (non-threatening) queer, when I assimilate and prove I'm just like them—because my goal is to rework the framework through which we think, feel and live sexual difference rather than simply expanding the category of "normal." I also make sure that my students are aware not to tokenize—that there are many different kinds of queer individuals, just as there are many different kinds of heterosexual individuals.

It would not be unlikely that because of the very nature of the material I teach, students would be very aware of not only their own bodies in the classroom, but that of their instructor's. There is immense potential productivity of my sexual body/identity in disrupting students' ideas of identity formation and categorization. Because our bodies are constantly being read by our students, we can use that opportunity to show them how identities (in this case sexual identities) are constructed, fluid and flexible, rather than essential, stable, fixed and immutable. As I share my sexual identity with my class and discuss the ways in which it has been formed and performed, I will ask my students (some of whom will inevitably be heterosexual) to do the same! "Coming out," therefore, is an intentional pedagogical tool—a way of deconstructing previously conceived notions of (sexual) identity. Exposing that we all deploy multiple subject positions is critical in enabling students to queer their conceptions of gender and sexuality in relation to an understanding of the dynamic possibilities of their own bodies as sites that are continually being formed and performed and have the potential to do queer and/or feminist, activist work. Again, the goal is to break away from simple social reproduction, which is at the core of the institution of the school, as mandated, or should I say manipulated, by the State.

In closing, (of this paper, because this work, *my* work, is just beginning), I continue to explore the implications of my sexual self-disclosure and strive to break free from the public/private, mind/body dualism that has long dominated the institution of the school and conceptions of both the classroom space and the educator herself. I will continue to work through finding a balance of both safety and threat in my classroom and work to make my students think critically about my body and identities as well as their own, constantly questioning how we have come to form and know ourselves, and juxtaposed to/dictated by whom and to whose benefit/detriment.

Dear Diary:
A Narrative Journal of my First Years as a 'Fag Teacher'
Stacy Fox

❧

"Ms. Fox, can I ask you a personal question?"

It was the night before grades were due for the first marking period in my first year of teaching, at an inner-city public high school on Chicago's South side. I stayed entering grades until the building locked for the night, and I was a little anxious about leaving after dark in that neighborhood. There were about twenty students milling around outside after the "After School Matters" program when I left, and I had stopped to chat with a few of my students when another interrupted. I had never seen this girl before, but it had become normal to hear my name from the lips of students I had never met. The conversation stopped when I told her she could ask me anything she wanted.

"Is you gay?"

I should have been expecting it. My fourth day of teaching I was called a "dyke" in two separate classes, and the subject has come up at least twice a week in one way or another since. I allowed my honors class to choose their own topic for the persuasive essay our scripted curriculum said it was time to write, and two of my students chose LGBT topics: "Why gay marriage is wrong," and "Why being gay is a choice." I told them they could write about any topic as long as they were able to support their position with three strong main points. I conducted class discussions on all their topics (the rest of which were mostly anti-abortion and pro death penalty) in the most equal, unbiased way I knew how. I disagreed personally with nearly everything they said, but I did a good job of remaining a neutral party. Though only two of the topics centered on gay issues, the conversation gravitated toward these subjects much more often than the others. In other classes, I began to hear students debating my sexual orientation in the back of the room and in the hall. I was asked frequently if I have a husband or a boyfriend, how many kids I have, and how many I plan to have some day. I assume most of these questions are attempts to derail whatever class discussion I am trying to facilitate, and my usual responses are honest and brief. I follow them with a standard invitation to continue personal discussions after school, and move on with my lesson.

This cool night outside of the classroom, I had no lesson to hide behind. I was faced with a direct question I was not prepared for, and I had already promised her an answer. Though the topic seemed ever-present in my classes, no student had asked me about this directly. My stomach was in my throat. I had decided that I would not lie about the issue, but I had only a vague idea of what kind of an environment this school is for LGBT students and teachers. I loosened the scarf around my neck and tried to speak clearly. "It's not always that simple. Some people date men and women..." I left, running the exchange over in my head the whole commute home.

I have since learned of four gay teachers at my school, none of whom are out to their students, and only a couple of whom are out to select staff members. I spoke with one, a young female teacher in her fourth year there, about the school's environment. For all the violence in the halls and classrooms; for all the riots after fire alarms, neighborhood shootings, and general threats against staff and teachers, I have never felt unsafe at my school. I trust the metal detectors at the door, the police and security officers. I feel safe walking to and from my car. But Ms. W told me stories that day that made me wish I had answered that student differently.

When she first began at the school, Ms. W felt overwhelmed and intimidated by similar comments and conversations in her classroom. Being called a "dyke" and dodging marriage and family questions distracted from her classroom so much that she began wearing a fake diamond ring. She and her partner have a son, and she started talking about him more often to avoid suspicion. She told me there are virtually no openly gay students in the school, and about the treatment the few who were out had to endure, not only at the hands of students, but of the administration and security staff as well. A gay male teacher has been pushed up against the wall in the hallway, threatened, and pushed over a table by students. I have heard security guards joking with students about kids being "faggots" or "fruits." There was an openly gay boy a few years ago whom they let join the dance team, but prohibited from performing in front of other schools. Upon stepping on the floor at an in-school pep rally, the student body began chanting "Just kill yourself!" The administration did nothing. Once, when Ms. W was overheard talking about the incident, she was physically backed into a chair by a department head, warning her that if that boy "chooses to live like that," he needs to "accept what is coming to him," and that she needed to mind her own business.

Though she is not out to her students, Ms. W has stopped wearing the phony ring, and several students who are very likely gay have started hanging out in her room quite a bit over the last couple years. "They know, like I know," she says. "We don't have to talk about it until they're ready. They see my room as a safe place." She and I began talking privately about starting a GSA at our school. Weighing what that could mean for our jobs and our safety, we decided to proceed carefully, looking for a sizeable group of students, several more teachers, and documented parental support before we consider bringing the idea to our principal. Shortly after our conversation, a counselor approached us about the very same thing. A group of girls came to him for resources to start a "gay girls' group" at the school, and he asked if we would be interested in helping. Of course, we were. The girls named the group "Pride," and we have since held four meetings and one small field trip. It has been a hard thing to organize, and many members of staff have made it known that they don't approve, but so far nothing terrible has happened, and our principal even went so far as to commend us at an all-staff meeting for our efforts, which neither of us expected.

Statistically, about one hundred and fifty students at this particular school are dealing with the fear and silence of hiding or denying who they are. Currently (almost two years after beginning this narrative) we have ended our second school year with six regularly-attending members of "Pride." While I understand the many factors contributing to our low membership, I can't help being a little disappointed that we couldn't reach out to more of the student population. I am thinking of Elijah, the timid over-achieving freshmen who spent every lunch period in my room practicing his routine for the community dance group he was thrilled to have joined. It took seven and a half months, but he finally admitted to me one day the real reason he was crying in the stairway 4th period. We talked about the dynamic between him and his much-older boyfriend, the possible repercussions of his coming out to his father, and how lucky he is to have a couple people in his life he can talk to openly about this. Being the top student in his class and highly involved in student activities, he reacted just how I thought he would when I invited him to our Pride meeting that week. He saw association with the group as potential social suicide: "Maybe in a couple years, Ms. Fox, but right now I just need to survive being a freshman."

The group has grown, (albeit modestly,) and so have I. I decided before this school year began that I would answer all (appropriate) questions about myself just as honestly as any straight teacher would. When my partner asked me to marry her last Fall, I was comfortable telling my students about it when they noticed the ring on my finger, and the response was overwhelmingly positive. I have learned to take the bad with the good. With the homemade "Congrats, MRS. Fox!" cards came harassing phone calls and the occasional threat. With the rainbow tassels hanging from four square hats at graduation came Devon failing freshmen English because he refused to be taught by a "fag teacher."

There are days the world gets to us—that we let ourselves become convinced that the challenges of opening ourselves to the hundreds of young people we face each day is akin to walking through their broken neighborhoods at night, not questioning if you will be struck down, but when. Fortunately, even when all of those young people seem to turn on you, we are strong enough to remember that we have been a positive role model for at least ten percent of them, whether they realize it at age fourteen or thirty-seven. They will remember the person who showed them that gay does not mean stupid, inferior, or morally reprehensible. They will carry that with them, whether they like it or not.

Hey Virginia, What's the Writing on the Wall?
Jennifer Smith

୧୨

I remember reading Virginia Woolf for the first time in high school. The school itself was settled on the outskirts of suburbia, nestled on the line between society and empty paddocks. While the building itself was fairly small my old literature class was even smaller, just the ten of us sitting around old laminate-peeled tables while my teacher, Mrs. Mason, stared vacantly out the window, her hand lazily selecting new people to read aloud.

The book was *Mrs. Dalloway,* and those of you who have read it will know it is hard enough to read and follow by yourself, let alone when it's read aloud to you by semi-illiterate teenagers, reading with the same intonations as if they were reciting a shopping list. Even the most avid Woolf fan would find this experience obscenely dull. When the time came to discuss what most had only been pretending to listen to, there would inevitably be very little to say. Most weeks we found ourselves sitting around limply for the last half an hour of class, waiting desperately for the bell to ring, as our dull-eyed teacher listened to our attempts at discussion crumble into school yard hearsay and gossip. Occasionally she tried to nudge the conversation back to the books but, perhaps from too many years of blank faces staring back at her, most of these attempts were half-hearted to say the least.

"Can *anyone* think of any themes that one might see in *Mrs. Dalloway*?" she said, one hand clasping her pen like a cigarette.

Silence.

"Can anyone think of one? A theme, can anyone think of a theme...?"
Silence, followed by a dejected sigh.

"Really, just give it a go, anything that comes to mind when we think *Mrs. Dalloway.*"

"She was a lady," said a boy after a long pause. "So I guess there would have been a lot of... you know... lady themes."

"Yes, I suppose there would have. Thank you for that. And what exactly would you say these 'lady themes' are?"

James shrugged his shoulders, knowing he had done enough already to get his daily participation quota filled. More silence ensued.

I honestly used to believe that when Jane Austen said, "A *woman*, especially if she has the misfortune of knowing anything, should conceal it as well as she can," she was talking not only about 19th century society, but also of high schools in the 1990's. That particular day in Literature class is a perfect example. Perhaps I had been the only one conscious enough to have heard anything read that day, or perhaps I was genetically inclined to have plucked it out from all the dull murmurings; either way, when one of the girl's tedious readings expressed that Mrs. Dalloway felt about women "the way men feel" I heard it and I understood.

Just as Mrs. Mason's eyes glazed over, I suddenly found myself speaking up. Mrs. Dalloway liked girls and that surely had to be a theme. I knew that even if I didn't understand most of what Clarissa had been going on about, I could be sure that Mrs. Dalloway thought that Sally was wonderful and that she never really got over her.

"I'm pretty sure," I said, my words cut through the silence, "that Mrs. Dalloway was in love with Sally. And so one of the 'lady themes' would be that Mrs. Dalloway liked, well, ladies. Also I think she may have been a bit mad."

"She had to have been," a blonde girl in the back muttered.

"Good, good, keep going," said Mrs. Mason.

"I don't think she fully realized she was gay though, or maybe she did. I don't think you were allowed to be gay in those days."

"Would you say then that she's trying to discuss the shackles of hetero-normative society?"

"I think she was trying to plan a party for most of it..."

"No, no," Mrs.. Mason said. "While Woolf was discussing it, that amongst all the thoughts of the party, there were hidden mediations on the love of the Sapphos, the beauty of Lesbos."

A snigger arose from the class. Mrs. Mason's eyes fell on me. Did she *really* just say Lesbos? I thought. As everyone stared at me, I wished I had said nothing.

It had only been a few weeks since I made a narrow escape. There had been party, there had been a park, there had been a collection of small town teenagers with cheap *Passion Pop*, and there had been Liz. She had a nose that turned slightly up like a mouse, short dark hair, and could be most commonly recognized wearing an *Incubus* t-shirt and an infallible smile. It had been a good night—which was generally accepted to mean that someone got punched, many people "made-out" and that almost everyone would have angry parents waiting anxiously at doorsteps when they got home.

After the party a rumor started up at school that Liz had been seen with a girl, behind a cluster of trees that were not quite full enough to hide the two of them. Apparently they had their tops off, or their pants off. Some people even said they had seen them fucking, though when asked how exactly they "did" it, the supposed witnesses were at a lost to explain.

I could have explained: a red-faced kiss, with shirts and pants very much still on. A slight bit of bark rash on one arm from leaning so heavily against a tree trunk, but that was all, and I should know, I was there.

After that Liz was less known for her excellent choice of band t-shirts and instead was known for being our high school's first outed "dyke," or rather more creatively, "that-fucking-Lezzo."

It was odd to be sitting in the same yard, hearing the same words said and knowing that they only belonged to her. I am not sure why she never turned me in, but she didn't. I suppose that it was my lack of confession that had been the reason that I was never asked to kiss her again. I had wanted to, but the writing was on the wall—the toilet wall that is—and it said in many variations that "Lizzy Hayworth is a fucking dyke."

"You know what, *I have no idea what the book was about*," I said that day in class. "The whole thing could have been '*Lesbos*' for all I know, it was still a bit shit." I blushed while I said it, though I managed to announce it with enough zest to make some of the kids laugh and make Mrs. Mason's enthusiasm evaporate.

"Right then... well" said Mrs. Mason, "let's discuss this some more as a group. How do we think lesbian themes affected the novel as a whole?"

"Well, it made Virginia Woolf kill herself," said someone, pleased to at least know something vaguely related to something else.

"Yes, but Virginia Woolf just wrote it, she isn't actually Mrs.

Dalloway..."

"Yeah, but she did kill herself..."

"Yes, however ..."

"And she was a dyke too!"

"Jason!" scolded Mrs. Mason.

"What? She was!"

"Didn't Sylvia Plath kill herself as well?" A girl asked.

"I didn't know *she* was gay?" said another.

"For goodness sake, not all gay people kill themselves," Mrs. Mason yelped.

"Yeah, but, it wouldn't hurt if they did either," said a voice loudly from the back.

Once again there was silence, though this time even Mrs. Mason seemed to welcome it.

Alternatively, I first read *The Well of Loneliness* during my second year of university, in a small literature tutorial, where fifteen bored, almost-adults, sat around peeling laminate off tables. Our tutor stared vacantly out the window, waiting patiently for *someone* to say *something* about *anything.*

"Can someone tell me," the tutor asked, "about the themes in *The Well of Loneliness*? Come on, you are paying a lot of money for this, so you may as well at least *try* to learn something. Let's get a conversation going?"

"It's about lesbians," someone plucked from the top of their head. The tutor would sigh slightly at the painfully obvious answer.

Some things were very much like they were in high school. Yes, people were generally much more literate but certainly not more organized. Only half the people in tutorials would have read the novel the whole way through before coming to class and of those students, only one or two who could say something that wasn't a general re-cap of the plot. Still, at least you could be fairly sure when you went to the bathroom that your name wouldn't be scrawled derogatorily on the wall, or that if you did manage to think of something particularly insightful, perhaps something that could reveal something of yourself or your sexuality, that you could do so freely, with the only possible reproach being a waffling group conversation about who has or hasn't tried sleeping with someone of the same sex, or a story about a friend of a friend who's planning to go to California to get married.

From Classroom to Family
Sassafras Lowrey

ℰℛ

Where I come from there are no city names just county lines and roads without sidewalks or streetlights. In the county where I grew up you don't see gay people. Gay people were whispered about when our parents thought we were busy playing. Where I come from people smirked that Matthew Shepard got what he deserved when his body hanging on the fence came through satellite dishes onto our television sets. Where I come from you didn't see gay people, except for her. She was the high school journalism teacher, newspaper and yearbook advisor, photography teacher, and bulldagger. I remember watching her from my first day freshman year- before I'd come out to anyone, even myself. I watched the way she swaggered down the hallway between second and third period. Saw how her jeans were frayed at the bottom where they stretched down below the sole of her Doc Martin boots, how the back right pocket had a faded rectangle square of her wallet. I spent that whole year watching her, not understanding why.

My sophomore year I signed up for Stock's intro to journalism class. Her name was technically Ms. Stockton but everyone just called her Stock. It took three weeks for me to convince my mother that it would be okay for me to take the class. I was supposed to be a veterinarian, this class wasn't going to help me, it would be a waste of time, and finally ultimately, the truth of why she didn't want me there stumbled out. She didn't feel comfortable with me taking a class from "that teacher." My whole life I'd been a good girl. I'd gone to church, followed my parents' rules, and submitted to their abuse. I'd never talked back. Fighting to be in that class, to be near another dyke was my first act of rebellion.

I came out over summer vacation between my junior and senior years. No longer did I want to drive with my best friend out to the barn to watch her ride her horse. Instead I started hanging out with two boys who snuck into the closest city and went to underage clubs, who wore makeup, who were the school fags. When I came out that summer, telling the boys, deleting the search history on my computer so my mother wouldn't see, the only person I wanted to tell was Stock. I knew that she would understand. I counted the days until summer vacation ended.

Fear got the best of me and I avoided her for the first two weeks of school. I had bigger problems. My mother had found out. I'd always been a good girl, but no matter how hard I'd tried, I'd never truly been able to please her. The week after school started things unraveled. My mother pled guilty to felony assault of a minor, her daughter, me. I went back into the closet and went to live with adult friends, even deeper in the country. I avoided Stock in the hallways because seeing her made me ache for freedom that I'd only just tasted on my lips in the weeks I'd been out to friends, before my mother knew.

Before long the pull of queerness was too much. I caught sight of her outside the cafeteria. In an instant I decided to skip my senior seminar class and followed her inside. She was seated at a long table, supervising a rowdy study hall, a few of the students were busily doing homework while the rest played cards, did each others' makeup, or boasted about the weekend's party. I sat down across from her and pretended to be looking for some papers in my backpack.

I said hello but was surprised that when she looked up, it didn't seem like she was surprised to see me. The truth came tumbling out. I saw the ache in her eyes; she knew the life before me in that county, in that school would never be easy. She told me that it was dangerous for us to talk, and yet she did not send me away. She risked her job, confirming that she was a lesbian, talking of how the principal and superintendant had sat her down in a meeting telling her that if she ever referred to her partner as anything other than a roommate her job was gone, and they would make sure she never worked again. In the weeks that followed I became more brazen. I demanded the school let us form a gay straight alliance, threatened to sue if they didn't. I might have returned to the closet, to move in with those adult friends, but I'd forgotten to close the door and it wasn't long before they packed my belongings in garbage bags.

The day they kicked me out, Stock gave me her home phone number. It was the first time I'd ever seen her look truly helpless. We were sitting in her empty classroom; I sat on top of one of the student desks trying not to cry. I knew I could spend the night with a friend, but after that I had no idea what was going to happen. She asked if I had money for dinner and I nodded. She got up and closed the door and handed me her phone number. She told me to only call if it was truly an emergency, and then she apologized. She apologized for the way the world was, and told me that all she wanted to do was put me in her jeep and take me home. She wove a fantasy about how her partner would cook us dinner, and I could stay in the guest room. The reality was doing any of that would cost her job. She slammed her fist down on the Formica desktop and began ranting. If she were straight, if I were straight, there would be no problem with her taking me home. That night, curled up on a friend's couch, I thought about the guest bedroom at Stock's house and how I wished I were there instead. The rest of my senior year I made it a point to be as flamboyantly gay as I could. I cut my hair, dyed it purple, started wearing workpants and flannel shirts. My backpack was covered with rainbow patches, and queer buttons. If I was stuck finishing school in that county I was going to make every day a pride parade.

There were consequences for being out. Stock told me there would be and she was right. Nearly everyone in the school stopped talking to me. I got assaulted by one of the football players leaving AP Government. I carried a stack of GSA posters with me at all times because the minute I went to class after leaving one hanging in a hallway, it would be ripped down or defaced. The last month of school I was able to rent a small basement room in the city. I commuted three busses and two hours each way to get to school. I didn't feel safe staying out there anymore, constantly looked over my shoulder when I heard the revving of an engine behind me.

Stock supported me moving away, so long as I promised that I wouldn't stop coming to class and that I would make it to graduation. On some level though, I think she was sad to watch me leave rural life behind and head to the city, but she knew I couldn't be safe there. I'd broken the unspoken rule of being gay in that county, I was too out.

In the weeks before graduation we fought over if the GSA could appear as a student club in the yearbook. I was shocked that she would protest. In the city I was attending protests, and doing community organizing. Being surrounded by queer people and not fearing for my safety was becoming a norm. It wasn't until she sat me down and said how scared she was that I remembered that as yearbook advisor our presence in the book held consequences for her too. The world might be changing, the school had no choice but to allow us to start the club or risk legal action, but they still held power. In a secret meeting the principal had explicitly forbidden her from being our faculty advisor. In the end she and I worked out a compromise: only seniors would appear. There were three of us and we were all leaving the county. It would be too dangerous for the handful of underclassman to be pictured with the club, because they would have to walk down those hallways come September. Unlike the equestrian club or earth club, the principal made everyone get parental permission to appear in the yearbook. I'd been on my own all year. I signed my own waver with purple ink, daring the principal to challenge me. Stock took our photo after school in the lobby of the building.

In the months after I graduated, Stock became more than a former teacher; she and her partner became my adopted family. They provided me with an unconditional support system that has continued to this day. I was always a good student, but school was never easy for me. I was an outcast as far back as I can remember. The taunts of my queerness began in early elementary school, long before I even knew the meaning of "dyke" or "lezzy." I dreaded going to school and facing the torment of my peers day after day, especially in high school, and particularly after I knew just how different, just how queer I was compared to everyone around me. Stock was my life preserver. She was more than a teacher to me. She was proof that it was possible to have the sort of life that until then had only existed in my fantasies.

Stock would sneak me copies of the local gay and lesbian paper from the nearby city. I carried those precious queer words hidden in my backpack. Despite being an honor roll student, were it not for her classes my senior year there is little doubt in my mind that I would have dropped out. There were some days that seeing her was the only thing that got me out of bed and onto the bus at 5 a.m. She taught me to keep my head up while walking through the hallways, while walking through life, no matter what slurs are being slung. Stock taught me how to write my first story, how to take a good picture, but most importantly she taught me how to survive as a woman, as a dyke in school, in a county, and in a world that didn't value us.

The Queerosphere: Musings on Queer Studies and Creative Writing Classrooms (*On Poetry, Creativity, and the Fleetingness of Things*)
Maureen Seaton

ℰℐ

For Steve Butterman and his extraordinary students

1.

Whenever I think of the Queerosphere I think of the first time I went to my friend Steve's Queer Studies class and I was a big queer about to talk about queer queer queer. I wasn't *too* self-conscious, with a Big Q carved into my forehead and Queen Latifah tattooed on my right ankle. No, really, my first time in Steve's classroom I was nervous because I was no longer with the woman I'd been with in the book of poems his students had just finished reading and were going to ask me questions about and that just seemed wrong. (Steve has his students make up questions, and unlike a lot of students in other classrooms in other places, they actually do make up questions.) Now I've been to Steve's *queerospheric* classroom (a term he made up) many times, and I think of his students with great warmth. In fact, these musings could be called "Steve's Students," because it is about them, really, at the heart—all of their faces turned upward with what I can only call queer anticipation.

2.

With my own student poets I am less comfortable being that queer. It's because I'm afraid of stepping on their toes and/or eliciting responses of not exactly homophobia but something more like a judgment that might sound like this: *That queer only wants to teach us about other queers.* I know, this isn't giving my students a lot of credit, but I have to admit I have trouble when anyone's curriculum, including my own, is heavily weighted in any direction. Right now I'm not talking about a Queer Studies classroom, but a Creative Writing classroom, so my mind is a bit confused, which I actually take to be the first step in either the queer impulse or the creative writing impulse—any impulse that ends in creating anything, in fact. So perhaps my confusion is seeking an answer and perhaps there is an answer, and my queer impulse, which gets mixed up with my creative writing impulse, which is okay, really, is seeking this particular answer. But answers seem anti-queer unless they are simply lighted upon for a second, a proboscis extended into the flower's honey, and then the creature moves on. My classroom is not a queer studies classroom, yet I am a study in queer. Steve's classroom is a queer studies classroom and Steve is also a study in queer. We've known each other a while now. We both like to create things and we both like to eat. We both like to look at lakes (which we're doing right now) and we both like to fly, but not in planes. Steve's students love me for being their queer guest writer. My own students have more ambivalence about me because to them I am like a teacherly mother of some sort and they actually don't like to think of me having any sex at all, with anyone.

3. ...*in constant motion/mutilation*

This phrase interests me and it raises another memory from the Andy Goldsworthy documentary Steve and I just watched where the sculptor talks about destruction. I'm all for destruction as a part of creation. So constant motion must mean mutilation, although the word destruction appeals to me a little more than the word mutilation because mutilation seems to come from without, whereas destruction, to me, can come from within. Am I judging that? One of the basics I embrace is "Don't judge." Also: "Don't limit." This may make me more queer than who I sleep with, certainly, and perhaps extremely queer in the way I create and teach, because if all is in constant motion, which it is (and we are), then nothing can be judged because nothing stays itself long enough to be judged. Or analyzed. Well, anything may be judged or analyzed, but perhaps it is queer to remember that one is only analyzing a certain iteration of a certain thing (or a certain person) that exists in a single moment of time and space. Speaking of Fernando Pessoa (which Steve and I were doing a few minutes ago), I would love to be able to wrap my mind around the idea of a poet writing extensively in more than seventy-two personas. (Pessoa called them his heteronyms.) I'd settle for the ability to write as even one other person. I do often speak in parentheticals, which could be a sign of someone lurking. (A woman just walked by with beautiful hair. Maybe her.) What does this have to do with teaching?

4.

I guess there are many ways to and around the pedagogy of poetry. A wise lesbian once suggested to me that poetry was not generally accessible simply because its ideas had not been thought of yet by the general population, that its nature was of "one who has yet to come." (Quotes mine.) In this way it spearheads creativity and perhaps culture itself, leading us forward through its images and metaphors. This consoled me then and it consoles me now but has little (?) to do with our topic of the day, which is about the queerospheric classroom. I would say that poetry is not inherently a queer literary genre but that because poetic license exists even in the mind of the general population as an accepted possibility, poetry lends itself to a queer literary genre a bit more than the others. I'm troubled by theory, but that would be like saying I'm troubled by the message of Christ or the teachings of Buddha or the way Isis mothers us or Moses leads us into the cooperative sea. And I am. There's a coot moving across the lake now. I am like him in that I am moving like a shadow across a larger body than mine, because I am dedicated to the other side of the lake and therefore preoccupied with my vision. This is where my life resembles the life of Mary Shelley, the way she sat down with a few friends one night and said, "Let's see who can write the scariest story ever written." I am like that about so many things, trying to scare myself and everyone else with my inability to paddle in a straight predictable line.

5.

It's like watching a person move from the sun to the moonlight, no, vice versa—there is a shift, who cares in which direction? Neither is elite, neither from a place of sore loser. I can't ever remember when I was sure. I've been so queer for so long I can't remember any other name besides

Slim Shaky. (This is not a heteronym, Steve, please don't expect a letter from Slim anytime soon.) Am I hopelessly unable to write analytically at this point? Do I want to do that in this piece of writing that borders on the prose poem? The prose poem, now there's a queer genre, if ever. Yet it seems to have been appropriated quite solidly by straight white men, which is okay, isn't it? Was Baudelaire gay? Rimbaud? Stein? I want to stay here now, sitting in the sun until my vitamin D level rises above sea level. Why are the gulls upset? How do I know they're upset? Am I frustrated because I haven't written a damn thing from my left brain all day and my right brain is mutating with each stroke of the keys. No. It is all the same, all light and all the moon's umbra. Who else is so lucky they get to do this, sit and feel this thin soft moment? What is queer about the classroom is that it is always moving like those coots, those gulls, that it defies definition but not in a defensive way. It simply falls through the fingers like lake water. Organic. Authentic. Is this too much to want? Is *queering* a fractal situation or do fractals live deep in the bodies of queers as they live in anyone? That is the joke *and* the bible story—the truth, you might say, if there was such as thing as truth, if there was such as thing as you.

Jensen Beach, Florida
March, 2010

My Battle Armor
Liz Matelski

❡

As a graduate student, but also an undergraduate instructor of history, the first day of meeting a new group of students is always a little daunting. Even though I've taught enough courses to feel like a "veteran" by this point, the first day of school continues to hold a thrilling nervousness for me. Before I step into that classroom and feel their expectant eyes on me, a bevy of questions fills my head. Will they ask a question I don't know the answer to? Will they take me seriously even though I look the same age as them? Will they respect my authority in the classroom?

Although I'm nearly a decade older than most of my students, I can read the disbelief on their faces when I walk into the classroom on that first day and begin writing on the front chalkboard. Their expressions unanimously ask, "*You're* our teacher?"

And piled on top of this mountain of general anxieties not unique to graduate instructors is yet another private fear: will they know I'm gay?

I teach at a private, Jesuit-affiliated university. And although within my own graduate department, I've faced nothing but openness and kindness in regards to what goes on in my personal life, there's always an underlying unease when walking into a classroom that might not have a clock, but always contains a crucifix on the wall. I take for granted that my graduate advisors don't judge me for whom I date, but I become hypersensitive about having the students I teach find out I'm a lesbian.

I don't accept "Friend" invitations on Facebook from current students, I make sure my privacy settings are set to the highest level on all social networking sites, and I never talk about my personal life during class or in my office hours. And as the post-structuralist philosopher Judith Butler would say, I "perform" heterosexual.

One of the benefits of academia is we can generally look how we please and wear whatever clothes we want. With a Ph.D. in hand, no one worries about piercings or visible tattoos or urban-influenced haircuts, at least not in my history-teaching community. When *I* teach, however, I dress in skirts and knee-high boots. I fix my hair in long waves and wear make-up and contacts although I'm far more at ease with a ponytail, jeans, and reading glasses.

My teaching mentor, a tenured professor with a fondness for tailored suits and bowties, always told me he dressed to teach as though visiting a lover. At first I tried to convince myself that I was only dressing to impress, as he had instructed, and to set a boundary between my students and myself since we were only a few years apart in age.

But really, the way I dress and the make-up I wear is my battle armor against "detection." Femininity is my line of defense from unwanted discrimination. Some might call it "femme privilege" or "femme invisibility." She wears a skirt; therefore, she can't be gay.

Late in the semester of teaching my first undergraduate course, one of my students visited me during my office hours. I considered him to be one of my "better" students because he actively participated during class discussions and did excellent work on exams and essays, but we had never had a conversation outside of the classroom. I was a little surprised when he showed up at my office door because normally I only saw students who were struggling or who wanted to argue with me about a grade.

This student revealed to me that he was questioning his sexuality and was having a hard time dealing with the accompanying thoughts and emotions. To make matters more difficult, he was an active participant in the campus's Christian organization and worried that this might make him a hypocrite. Rather than reacting to his dilemma, my initial thought was, *Oh no. Everyone in class knows I'm gay. That must be why he's Coming Out to me.*

It never occurred to me until later in our conversation that he had no idea I was a lesbian. He had simply found me to be an open, compassionate person, and felt comfortable revealing this personal information with me.

I've never been guarded about being a lesbian; I literally "Come Out" to people I meet usually within the first few minutes of introduction, finding the opportunity to talk about some activity my partner and I did over the weekend. It's not generally a conscious thing on my part, but I've been burned in the past. Perhaps I now feel the need to lay my cards out on the table right away: "This is who I am. If you want to be my friend, you need to be okay with this."

And perhaps it's because of those past non-teaching-related situations that I'm guarded about my sexuality in front of a room of undergraduate students. I want my students to hate me because I'm a bad teacher. Not because I'm a lesbian. To clarify, it's not that I *want* my students to hate me or to think I'm a bad teacher. But if they don't like me, I don't want it to be about something I have no control over—like my sexuality.

I had a conversation with a number of female colleagues recently about the issue of teaching and identity. I wanted to know, how did they identify when they stood in front of a classroom? Universally, they all agreed that the number one "identity" of which they were acutely aware was their femaleness. In fact, one friend stated, "At no other time do I feel more female, or are more aware that I am a woman, as when I stand in front of a classroom full of students."

My own opinion differed slightly from my straight female friends, and I admitted that rather than teaching making me highly cognizant of my gender, I instead felt as though I had a secret and was hiding something important from the class. I wonder, however, if more than gender or sexuality, this is just a sense of vulnerability that young professionals feel when they are out numbered nearly 40 to 1 in a classroom. I wonder what my male colleagues would say if asked this same question about identity.

The main course I teach not only fulfills the general history requirements, but the diversity component as well at my university. Because of this, I have the opportunity to lecture on and assign readings about a variety of minority groups in American history. Among the various minority groups I cover in a semester, gays and lesbians are afforded two lectures.

No matter how many times I deliver these lectures, I always get nervous beforehand. It's almost the same amount of anxiety as before I give my "History of Abortion" lecture—which, as one can imagine, gets mixed responses from my students who attend a Catholic university.

I'm not normally a nervous person, but something about these lectures always makes my heart beat a little faster as I prepare.

The word "homosexual" gets stuck in my throat when I practice, the word feeling clinical and alien to my mouth. But how would students react if I used the word "queer"? Would they know it's *okay* to say that word when used appropriately? Or would they think their teacher is using slurs in her lectures?

Moreover, if I were Out, I question if students would see my GLBTQ lessons as a necessary addition to the syllabus or if because of my background, something I have added because I identify with that minority group. I often wonder if other history teachers from other under-represented groups feel the same way when they teach about the history of a minority group to which they belong.

We have a hard enough time in my discipline convincing undergraduates that the history course they're only taking to fulfill a general education requirement is relevant without a giant, rainbow hurdle to overcome as well. Although I should give my students the benefit of the doubt, I don't want to reveal my sexuality and have them tune-out and miss out on a course I believe to be instrumentally important to helping create responsible global citizens. Lofty? Yes. The study of history is that important.

But maybe these are all unfounded anxieties. Maybe undergraduate students are mature enough to take historical lessons at face value despite their own personal beliefs and backgrounds. And maybe the way I dress doesn't really matter. Maybe it's like Dumbo's magic feather and my outfit only gives me the mental ease that I will be treated just like any other young professional. And maybe one day when I'm a tenured professor with job security, having my students "like me" won't seem so important.

But until that day, I look in the mirror one more time before class, take a deep breath, and make sure my battle armor is in place.

We Weren't Queer Yet
Laura M. André

ೞ

My best friend Peter was furiously rocking to and fro in his chair, as he tended to do when he was nervous. My stomach was in knots. Had I just read what I thought I did? Another friend, Andy, was reading aloud as our raised-eyebrow glances ricocheted around the room. There was a huge elephant in the room as we sat in Judy Short's eleventh grade Honors English class, reading passages from *Moby Dick*: "Thus, then, in our hearts' honeymoon, lay I and Queequeg—a cosy, loving pair." We had already read about Ishmael and Queequeg sharing a bunk and Ishmael's "strange sensations" in response to Queequeg's hugging him in bed like a wife. Melville's novel was becoming increasingly intriguing.

Andy continued to read: "We had lain thus in bed, chatting and napping at short intervals, and Queequeg now and then affectionately throwing his brown tattooed legs over mine—." Andy stopped reading and raised his hand. He asked, "Does this suggest that they're...I mean, it seems very intimate...two men sleeping together, throwing their arms and legs around each other...Are they gay?"

We exhaled deeply. Finally someone gave voice to what we had all been wondering, but were too afraid to ask.

Judy Short stiffened. Her face grew taut and her eyes darkened as she stood up from behind her desk.

"How. Dare. You," Judy Short said. It came forth like a slow growl, growing in intensity and volume with each word. *"How dare you!"* she repeated, gaining momentum. And then again, as if Andy and the rest of us hadn't heard her the first two times, she said, "How dare you besmirch this great American literature with such...such"—she was literally stuttering and spitting by now—"a vile and contemptuous insinuation."

We were silenced. Judy Short told us that our minds were in the gutter—pervs!—and that we were wrong to think that Queequeg and Ishmael might have shared more than a platonic bed, wrong to think that Herman Melville himself might have known a little something about romantic love between men, wrong to think that we could've brought up such a topic in the classroom. Leaving aside the question of whether Melville was gay by today's standards, no explanation ensued about what it means to judge 19th-century social practices by 20th-century standards.

It was Kansas in 1983, smack dab in the middle of the country, not even halfway through Reagan's first term. And when I tell my therapist this story today, she wonders what happened to the social movements of the 1960s and 1970s, in which gay and lesbian issues were supposedly brought closer to greater social acceptance. I remind her that it was also the era in which AIDS first became public knowledge. Rock Hudson was still alive, but he would soon suffer and die from the so-called "gay plague." There was a backlash, and we students had neither the courage nor the knowledge to stand up to Judy Short, who, instead of raging, should have found a teachable moment in Andy's query.

The whole incident became something of a running joke among my group of friends, who found a way to inject humor into almost any situation by using the phrase "How dare you." We thought Judy Short must have been a very sexually repressed English teacher not to see what we took to be obvious gay content. (And she was a bit of a hothead, as evidenced several months later in another famous episode, when she dragged poor Janie Thompson—alone—out into the hallway to finish discussing Faulkner's *Light in August*, because Janie apparently was the only person in the class who had managed to read the darn thing.)

The not-so-funny part of things is that at least three of us in that classroom were totally shamed that day, our minds closed to the possibility of acknowledging a queer presence in our "great American literature" class. And then there was Judy Short's hostile and unapologetic disapproval of homosexuality itself. We didn't know what we were missing; that a nascent queer studies movement was gaining energy in universities all over the country, where scholars and students were actively discussing the very kinds of questions Andy raised.

Looking back over a span of nearly 30 years, it's clear that part of the reason that event resonated with me (aside from the classroom's shared trauma), was that it dealt a blow to my early queer sensibilities, which were just beginning to form. My stomach tightened up reading those passages from *Moby Dick* because I recognized something of myself in them. Ishmael's initial horror at having to share a bed with the "cannibal" Queequeg was motivated by racial difference rather than sexual sameness, but I read into the text this other layer of meaning. When Ishmael's resistance turns to pleasure, my heart began beating faster. Here, I thought, was an actual instance of elusive same-sex love in literature, and I felt the shock of recognition.

It would be another five or six years before, one by one, Peter, Andy, and I would come out. In 1991 I was sitting in a coffee shop in Los Angeles with Peter when he said out of the blue, "Well, you might as well know that although I've sampled from both sides of the menu, so to speak, I'm in a relationship with a man." I was completely unsurprised by his revelation, but I was stunned by how long it took. I then told him that my "friend" and I were more than friends, and he—with his signature quick wit—said, "How dare you!" We laughed; he wasn't surprised, either. We both always knew, but never talked about it over the course of a decade during which we came of age. It was an anticlimactic, long-overdue coming-out for both of us.

One of the reasons why we remained closeted for so many years when, in retrospect, we knew we were gay or lesbian back in high school, was linked to the fact that we were not exposed to queer lives in literature and art; in fact, gay and lesbian themes were actively suppressed by the likes of Judy Short. There's a fear on the right that teaching gay/lesbian/queer issues will just "turn" straight students gay, which is of course hogwash. But maybe a closeted gay or lesbian person will be triggered to confront his/her sexuality by seeing it expressed in art. That's what happened to me; I wasn't fully out until I was exposed to gay/lesbian/queer studies in graduate school.

After graduating from high school, I went to a large state university, where I was in a sorority. Sexuality beyond the hetero variety was strictly forbidden, and we acted as if it didn't exist at all. I was deeply closeted and struggled mightily with my feelings. Again, none of my classes reflected the growing field of gay/lesbian/queer studies. I wish I

had a course catalog from those years, so I could see the kinds of courses
I could've taken. I never took a Women's Studies course. I was afraid
of the lesbian graduate students. They all seemed to be big dykes with
buzz cuts and I was terrified of them — terrified that I might become like
them. I wish I could've learned from them, though, and I was secretly
envious when I overheard their impassioned conversations on campus.

I tried about five majors throughout my undergraduate career, always
seeking a curriculum where some part of me would be reflected.
I quizzed out of college-level English, which was too bad, because I
think that was one department in which I could've learned something
about queer studies. Instead I took courses in chemistry and physics
and aerospace engineering, where class time was focused on explaining
rules rather than finding exciting situations in which the usual, assumed
heteronormative rules didn't apply.

But my interests began to shift, much to my conservative father's
horror, towards the humanities about my junior year. I began taking
courses in art history and film studies. I remember getting really turned
on by Bergman's *Persona* in my foreign film class. Our discussions in
that class, however, were all about camera angles, lighting, and editing,
and not one word about the intense relationship between the women
on screen. Likewise, in my art history courses, little did I know that
scholars elsewhere were charting gay and lesbian presences across the
history of western art; it just wasn't taught at my university. Not at the
undergraduate level, at least.

But in the following years — it was the mid-1990s by now — I
gradually became aware that the kinds of things I wanted to study
were staples of the curriculum in art history graduate school. I was also
beginning to acknowledge my sexuality at this time, but I wasn't quite
queer until I went to graduate school and I was able fully to come out
to my friends and (initially horrified) family, not to mention myself.
I think this has to do with having the language and legitimacy to be
more open about my sexuality. Graduate school was like a flowering
of intellectual and creative energy for me. I devoured books by Eve
Kosofsky Sedgwick and Judith Butler. Prior to having that academic
legitimacy, my sexuality seemed to not exist.

Andy, Peter and I came out not during high school, but rather years
later after college and/or grad school had steeped us in a language that
made it possible and meaningful to say "I am queer." It was a process
of owning and naming a sexuality that was connected to a valid

discourse, not just the emotional reactivity we experienced when we were younger, and, arguably, not quite queer yet. I often wonder how it would have been different had I not gone to graduate school. What catalyst would have propelled me out of the closet? Given the timing, Ellen might have been my eventual trigger, but what would that have looked like and how would I have managed the process of coming out as a result of a pop culture phenomenon? Had I not gone to graduate school, however, the second part of my story, in which I transitioned from queer student to queer teacher, wouldn't have happened.

After I earned my Ph.D., I was fortunate enough to get a tenure-track job and a contract for a book with a major university press known for its theoretical and cultural studies-based booklist. I taught courses in the history of photography, and I made sure that my courses included gay/lesbian/queer themes. I also taught courses in lesbian art and culture and queer visual culture. I was no longer the high-school student who'd been shamed. I had complete academic freedom. But you know what? Those latter courses were a dud. The self-selecting students already knew all about queer theory, and gay and lesbian studies, and homophobia, and, while they were eager to learn about new artists and films, they had a somewhat blasé attitude about the whole thing. As if they were cooler than the class was. Perhaps it was my fault; I'm not averse to taking the blame for what turned out to be anti-climatic courses, where there was little real discussion because everyone was already on the same page. But active discussion wasn't a problem in my other classes, so I had to take a hard look at the content that produced such a disinterested response from my students.

I became ambivalent. I wondered, how far can we take queer theory and/or gay/lesbian studies? Eradicating homophobia like Judy Short's is a worthy cause, and I often wonder if she's still teaching, and if so, what she's teaching. But I didn't have success teaching gay/lesbian issues to my students. My classes were full of eager students, but my heart wasn't in it. I could never get beyond the "Duh, they're gay, so what?" attitude. Of course some lesbian artists feature lesbian themes in their work. I was a bit of a failure at teaching it, but that doesn't mean I have stopped believing in the value of teaching it.

In my own research, however, I had another problem. I had written a dissertation about the visual culture of the space-age 1960s, and being in grad school, I had attached a lot of importance to queer theory. I was "queering" the space age, with all its difference and the cultural movements of the time: black power, the women's movement, gay liberation, together with the far-out nature of space travel. It just seemed really queer. Plus, I was exploring the conflation of my father's "square" space-age values (he was a test pilot in the 1960s—and an astronaut candidate) with my own, much more radical ones. My father, whose values had moved a bit to the left since I came out, actually approved of my endeavor.

But the more I worked on my book, the less I believed in it. I balked at the idea of making it a "queer" book, as if queer theory were a commodity that I was expected to cash in on. It was the sexy topic *du jour*, and in the academic space race, queer theory was the rocket I was trained to fly. It went from being something I couldn't talk about in high school to the only thing I was supposed to talk about. I didn't (and don't) believe that the moon, or outer space, is queer, as both my very smart dissertation advisor and successful editor encouraged me to assert. The moon is wildly different from Earth, and there are some very queer things about the space age, but I was at an impasse as far as turning the whole thing into a cohesive narrative arc. Ultimately I walked away, and left the book unfinished.

I can't help but think about how far things have come, between what happened that day in Judy Short's class to the kind of academic freedom I had and practiced at my teaching job. I enjoyed teaching immensely, and my classes were popular. But alas, teaching wasn't the only part of the job. I also had to publish. My book wasn't going to happen, so I did a thing that almost nobody does: I left a tenure-track job voluntarily. I went from not being queer yet in one classroom to not being queer enough in another.

Now, some say, queer theory is in a state of decline, due to a greater mainstream acceptance and understanding of homosexuality. It's similar to those who argue that the women's movement is essentially over because women are better off now than they were 40–60 years ago. This kind of thinking espouses insane arguments like the one that says, "Look, gays are now on television, for god's sake. We don't need same-sex marriage."

I've been on both sides of the classroom. As a student being largely ignorant of queer issues, to the professor teaching students who already know about queer issues—there's a major sense of progress in those 25 years. It's testament to those who began writing queer lives and questioning literature and visual art in the early 1980s, when I was just a teenager in Kansas.

My queerness had much to do with my teaching and research—perhaps too much to do with it. I could've produced the book that led to tenure, produced something to get along; but I couldn't escape the whole "emperor's new clothes" vibe. In order to be true to myself, I had to give up teaching. I had to come out again, this time as someone who wasn't so sure about the intellectual foundation of her work. So I decided to let it go, for the whole project to rest in a box, like the boxes of moon rocks underground at the space center in Houston. As far as fusing my father's space-age values with my own queer space age goes, it was a near miss. And I wasn't willing to force them to meet, so I walked away. And perhaps that's the queerest thing I've ever done.

Mr. Short Hair
Jessica Gardner

CO

After work, I headed for the bus. From behind, I heard, "Mr., Mr., Mr. Tie, Mr. Short Hair!" I recognized the high squeaky voices, partially muffled by braces, and the hoard of giggles that followed. It was my fan club, as I like to call them. My fan club consists of a group of twelve to fifteen-year-old girls who follow me out of work on a semi-regular basis. Though we have never actually interacted, I am often privy to their deeply philosophical debates (last week it was: out of all of his girlfriends, who does Andrew like the most?) and conversations, mainly because they are intentionally spoken within range. Normally, as my luck would have it, these conversations focus around me. They almost always fall back to debating whether I am actually a woman, and usually the merits of my womanhood, or manhood as some days would have it, are based on my attire. Today, they noted, I happened to be looking extra "faggy." Black button up shirt, sweater vest, tie, black skinny leg trouser pants, and some Sperry Sidewinders. Complete with black Diesel watch and, as it was drizzling when I left, fitted LA Dodgers cap. Normally I take being called faggy as a huge compliment. I mean, androgyny is hard work, and it definitely isn't cheap! However, in the context of my "fan club," and my work in general, it's hard to see it as anything other than your run of the mill, daily dose of middle school homophobia.

To explain why my life revolves around teenagers, and to put this essay in context, let me explain my job. I am a middle school special education teacher at a very large public middle school in the Bronx, New York. I have successfully completed two years at this school, and I will happily be returning in the fall for my third year, much to my California-based family's chagrin. I did not plan on being a teacher and previous to two years ago, I had taken no steps or training to ensure this outcome. Upon graduating from Stanford University in 2008, I was recruited by Teach for America. I do not wish to go into an analysis of educational efficacy and Teach for America, as it is not the focus of these musings, but to understand future references, you have to have some background. Teach for America is a non-profit aimed at eliminating education inequalities and ensuring that every child has the right to an excellent education. To achieve this, the organization recruits from top colleges and trains teachers to be placed in high-need, low income, community schools. Basically...to put us where not many others want to go. The commitment to the organization is two years, with the option of staying in education or moving to other sectors upon completion of your spell. For reasons still partially unclear to myself, after my second year, I made the decision to stay in the classroom for the long haul.

During our Teach for America boot-camp training, they touched on the subject of diversity in the classroom, with LGBT issues falling under that umbrella. However, after walking into the classroom, no amount of training would have been sufficient. My first year I taught an eighth grade bilingual self-contained special education class. This means that I had twelve students between the ages of twelve and seventeen, with differing language abilities, and disabilities ranging from emotionally disturbed to mentally retarded (yes, that's the actual education/medical classification). I had one paraprofessional in the room for assistance. School started at 8 a.m. By 9:30 a.m. on my first day I had been called "dyke," "fag," "homo," and, my personal favorite, "*marica*." It took me a few days and an awkward conversation with my assistant to figure out what that last one meant. That day I learned that I work in a "pick your battle" type of environment. I mean, when you're dodging desks and left-hooks, insults are the least of everyone's worries, including your own. Initially, at least, that's how I saw it and, I assumed, that's how everyone else saw it too.

The first year was exacting, mainly because I wasn't prepared. I mean, academically speaking, I was on top if it. I had the plans, the differentiation, the data that told me I was doing things right. Instructionally, I was leak-proof. However, in every other respect of what it means to be a teacher, a leader, and a human being in general, I was a sinking ship. I had NO idea how to deal with the tantrums, outbursts, fights, racism, sexism, homophobia, and every other insulting factor that these kids flung out like it was nothing. It was hard to build an overall classroom culture of respect when I, as the leader in the room, was the most disrespected person in there. That first year I didn't even dress "faggy," as the kids would say! I even wore a few dresses here and there, and I definitely never suited up a tie. Coming from living in a queer co-op on a college campus, where my main staples were jeans and black v-necks, professional dress was new to me and I went by what I saw, however uncouth it felt. But those kids must have had the most finely tuned gaydars, because they wouldn't let it go. The kids constantly asked me if I had a boyfriend, was married, had a girlfriend, lived with anyone, and a thousand other things that if answered directly and honestly, would have taken us into a grey area. A gay area.

Many people say that teachers shouldn't come out to students. A classroom is for learning, and talking about your personal life is inappropriate. This is why I refer to it as a grey area. I spend approximately six hours a day with the same twelve kids. And while the focus of that day is on education and learning, that also encompasses social learning. Because of the range of disabilities in the class, we often have to spend time working through personal issues before we can even pick up a pencil. I ask them to trust me. I ask them to confide in me. I ask them to let me in. I ask them to let me help. That in turn, means that we have some sort of personal relationship. Naturally, that needs to be two-sided for us to get anywhere productive. They want to know who I am. They want to know what my "deal" is. How can they trust me if they don't know me? And that is where it gets complicated.

Most teachers have pictures of their kids, husbands, wives, friends, significant others on their desk. They think nothing of wearing a wedding ring. However, looking "faggy" means that doing any of those things brings us into the grey "gay" area. No one would think twice if a female teacher told her class she was married (to a man). Yet, if I were to tell my class that I was married to a woman, my professional integrity would be in question. And to be honest, it sort of makes sense. When you tell someone you're gay, it automatically brings up the issue of sexual preference. It brings up sex. I don't want my students to associate me and sex AT ALL. That first year I avoided the topic at all costs. Change the subject, change the setting, change me.

I never thought clothes could mean so much. But, in middle school, one off-brand outfit for one unlucky student meant the biggest catastrophe imaginable. Anyone who works with youth knows what I'm talking about. That is why in my second year, however superficial and trivial it may sound, I realized that how I dressed actually affected how I was perceived by my students. Now, more confident in my classroom management abilities, I dressed how I felt comfortable. I basically looked like the men's department of Urban Outfitters threw up on me. That, combined with my Justin Bieber haircut and tattoos, for all intensive purposes, meant that I had decided to be a visibly gay presence at the school.

The beginning of the year, per tradition, saw insults and school supplies being thrown every which way. They didn't know me and therefore didn't like, trust, or respect me. Yet pretty soon we had come to some basic form of mutual respect. For the first few months, none of my students asked if I was gay. Actually, none of them asked me the entire year. They asked why I wear ties, why I have short hair, why I skateboard, why I look like a boy, why I don't have a boyfriend, why I'm not married, but no one directly asked the big question. I think no one ever directly asked me because they thought I would be offended and they didn't want to insult me. Perhaps, in a misguided way, this was a sweet sentiment.

What I found particularly hard to handle was the fact that the word "faggot" was reserved for the most intense displays of hatred. You know, there were the typical fights with "bitch" and "retard" being called, but I knew it was more serious as soon as I heard the word "faggot." That meant someone was about to have a meltdown. "Faggot" was the most insulting and terrible thing they could think of, and there was nothing the other person could say to top it. We addressed the issue loads of times, going over the etymology of the word, thinking about how you use it, about what it actually means, but in the heat of the moment, it still rang out as the mother of all insults. What was weird was that when they called each other faggots, they apologized to me afterwards. For example, as a fight was brewing one day, a student said, "Go suck a dick you fucking faggot. Sorry Ms. Gardner." What do I do with that? Don't apologize to me! Apologize to the millions of people you just insulted! Apologize to the person you are actively trying to hurt! Apologize to your family for making them look ignorant! Apologize to our community for making it unsafe! Apologize to the two kids in the class hurting under the weight of hiding who they are!

Even after my small breakthroughs last year, I still don't have a handle on how to address the issue of homophobia in the classroom. I do, however, strongly believe that it needs to be addressed and not ignored. I understand that there are many important things that need to be covered (like being twelve and not knowing how to read), but how is hatred not on the top of the list? As much as I would LOVE, LOVE, LOVE to say, "Hey, we can't talk about this right now, our New York state exams are next month (and after all, my professional abilities are being judged by your scores)," it unfortunately doesn't work that way. It can't work that way if we expect to have functioning learning environments. It can't work that way if we expect to live in a society where fundamental rights aren't denied, where people aren't emotionally and physically abused, and where you are not made to feel less than human because of who you are. Because of who you love. As I experience this topic personally and through my students, I'll continue to wear my rainbow Silly Bandz and address the issue honestly, with an open mind and an open heart. I mean, after all, in the words of my fan club, "Everyone's a silly faggot nowadays anyway."

The Week Matthew Shepard Died
Bonnie J. Morris

ℰℑ

October 11, 1998: National Coming Out Day

Tonight marks ten years since the first "National Coming Out Day," which began as a way to commemorate the 1987 March on Washington. I'm still incredibly excited to be part of the movement, and call my parents to thank them for their years of love and support.

October 12

But on the news, now, is the announcement about Matthew Shepard's death. And I am angry. ANGRY. Why has this country failed to make gay-bashing *unacceptable*? For a young man to be killed on Coming Out Day is symbolic of our national failure to protect gay youth. And I toss and turn all night in rage, rage, rage, rage, rage.

October 13

No more drowsy mornings; there's work to do out there in Homophobic Nation. How should I behave in class? I give a midterm to 120 women's history students, their pens and pencils scratching, scratching, my fine silk shirt soaked through with the sweat of grief. On my university e-mail: dozens of announcements about the candlelight vigil being put together for Matthew. One such e-mail begins, "Hello, Gentle People."

October 14

Focus. Describe. All day long I think of nothing but the lynching in Wyoming. All day, getting work done but thinking of Matthew Shepard: in my aerobics class, jump-starting my car, returning a lost bank card left by a Frenchman in the ATM, mailing law school references for my students—all day my mind is on the lynching. I write pages and pages and pages in my journal. "See you at the vigil?" someone says to me from a tear-blotched face. Just before heading out to attend the vigil at the Capitol, I go home and unwind by watching "Ellen" reruns on the Lifetime channel. In an unbelievable act of timing, the famous, hour-long "coming out" episode just happens to air today. Should I laugh or cry? I laugh and cry. Then I dress warmly, plaid flannel, black leather jacket, boots. Camera, journal, Metro fare, out the door in seconds, at the west Capitol steps in fifteen minutes.

Nine thousand people are gathered there. Angry sad faces, candles, signs. I have no idea what's planned, wiggle into the crowd, and listen to male politician after male politician whine at us, "Now is not the time for anger," while we yell "YES, IT IS." Congressmen from both parties make pious speeches about violence; Dick Gephardt and John Kerry are good, and Barney Frank, of course; but there is tension in the crowd when the Republicans speak. An older black woman actually grabs the mic and screams into it, "How dare you desecrate Matthew's memory with your politicking?" She's right: there's an election in three weeks: and we roar approval of her bold critique as security police wrestle her away. Now the politicians are suggesting that we pray, so much Lord and God in male language, and the crowd says no, no; that's part of the problem. Let us ACT. There's little mention of violence against women, as if lesbians are never attacked: what about Claudia Brenner, and the lesbians burned to death in Oregon? I perch halfway up a stone wall—ironic symbolism, stonewall—trying to see, scraping my shins, ankles and feet to shreds trying to see through an ocean of men's heads and asses. And suddenly Ellen DeGeneres walks in.

The crowd is screaming: ELLEN, ELLEN. She grabs the mic and bursts into tears. I am reeling—thoughts shoot along my neurons like Rice Krispies—just twenty minutes ago I was watching Ellen come out on television; and why is it that much spookier when *comedians* break down and cry? Ellen begins, "I am so pissed off. I can't stop crying." I am close enough to see that Ellen is reading a speech she ripped from a spiral notebook, curly schoolgirl edges and all; more than any other act, this makes her human, and the crowd is silent. "Just when they thought I'd do away," Ellen reminds us of her cancelled show; "I'm angry because *this* is what I was trying to stop. This is what I was trying to DO!" Fumbling with her spiral-notebook page, Ellen mixes up her words, sobbing: "I thought I knew what I wanted to say."

Now Anne Heche speaks. She is *phenomenal*, screaming at the religious Right: "I am so proud to be Ellen DeGeneres's WIFE. I DO NOT WANT TO BE LIKE YOU." Then Ellen's mom speaks, and as she becomes our symbolic non-rejecting mother we are ready to be led in prayer: the 23rd Psalm. At the line "He maketh me lie down in green pastures," though, we're all thinking of Matthew Shepard, made to die in a pasture. Then Kristen Johnson from "Third Rock From the Sun" speaks, raising her eyebrows at the press and saying "I was raised a white heterosexual Christian Republican, and I am so ashamed of my people—sorry, Daddy." The crowd is delirious; *these* women don't hold back. Kathy Najimy is also blazing onstage.

So many little kids here with their parents, just like I used to be in the 1960s, and a little girl asking, "What does DOMA mean?" and her gay father explaining. People are snarling at Connie Morella for voting in favor of DOMA [the Defense of Marriage Act] and then daring to show up here. I went to Walt Whitman High with her son, Mark; we sat next to one another in homeroom: Morella, Morris. My grades were better, but *his* rights are "defended."

I can't see anything. I swing over a wall, over some stairs, glad now for all those aerobics workouts. I sit on a step to relieve my cramped knees, and when I look up I am right next to Ellen and Anne. This is the media area. They're giving interviews to the press. I stay still as a mouse and watch everything. The tears roll down their faces; even their security guards are crying. Then Ellen's sad face changes totally when she smiles. It is hard not to be fascinated because, together, touching and stroking each other, they make an incredibly beautiful couple, and this is the real lesbian behavior that TV will not show. Kissing, hand-holding, anger. Matthew Shepard's closest friends Walter and Alex are there; they hug Ellen and Anne for a long time and cry. "Ellen! Ellen!" scream the onlookers before she is finally whisked off. "WE LOVE YOU, ELLEN!" Two big Capitol policemen standing next to me say to each other, "Damn. She *is* pretty."

A Human Rights Campaign staffer explains to me that the whole vigil was coordinated in just twenty-four hours, yet over fifty additional celebrities who wanted to speak had to be turned away.

A camera crew notices me clutching the railing and they ask *me* for an interview. I give them a good one; they're from Paramount. I identify my place of work, and say that I am out and proud and will come out, again, to all my new students.

The speeches last another four hours. I leave just before 11 because I want to see how this rally spins on the 11:00 news. In my apartment, I watch the news on four different stations, Ellen crying, Ellen and Anne. The great equalizer: we're all at risk, all ANGRY. At 1 a.m. I phone my parents in California and thank my mother for taking me to political demonstrations when I was a child. I describe the many parents, gay and straight, who brought their kids to the vigil at the Capitol and made them listen and understand. My mother tells me, "You keep fighting the good fight."

One-twenty in the morning and my internal life is roaring into overdrive: I'm planning to do a teach-in rather than lecture tomorrow; the power to affect 120 young people. I'm so excited I have to write in two different colors of ink. Wearing my best friend's old sweatpants, my father's old t-shirt; I need sleep! Sleep! But no. An autumn night at the Capitol, the dome lit up, flags blowing, candles flickering. Lights, camera, justice. Nothing is impossible; I can do so much.

October 15

Drained. Stunned. I slept fitfully from about 2:30 to 7, dreaming that a group of kids attacked me and threw dirt at me. I confronted them: "How do you think that makes me feel?"

How my shins ache from running on hard pavement, scaling walls. I call my first girlfriend from college days and thank her for being my first woman lover, for bringing me out when we were eighteen. She says, "You brought yourself out, woman. You were put on earth for a reason, to be an activist. I just happened to be there." I say, "But I'm glad it was you," and she adds, "Yeah, so am I, actually."

I go to school dazed, forgetting to brush my teeth, and with my underwear accidentally inside out and backwards. I write letters to three different newspapers. *The Washington Post* buries its report on page A7, while giving front-page coverage to a report on senior athletes and how they exercise. I'm livid—there were nine thousand of us! I have an e-mail from an ex in Colorado, who produces a gay cable show in Denver—she's just sent her camera crew to Wyoming for Matthew's funeral, and is hysterical with fear about the Fred Phelps hate group waiting to harass mourners.

At 2 p.m. I stride into my women's history class and cancel the regularly scheduled lecture. Instead, I talk about Matthew Shepard. I tell my one hundred and twenty first-year students that it could have been them—college students—or me—an out lesbian teacher. I come out to them all, though many knew or suspected, and we talk about the vigil, college students' vulnerability, the Biblical and cultural reasons gay people were first condemned in societies, the genesis of gay-bashing, the option of coming out to one's parents; I remind them that as voters they're empowered to uphold or *change* the status of my second-class rights as a homo. Two students are in naval ROTC uniform. What are they thinking? One whispers to his neighbor, "Will this be on the final exam?"

When the hour is up, many students come down to the podium and thank me, and others e-mail me later, expressing respect. The best surprise is a student I've never talked with before who follows me to the bus and says, "Listen, the women's rugby team would like to buy you a drink."

I race over to Georgetown University for my 4:15 class there, and give the same coming-out lecture, only with more attention to the crucifixion symbolism of Matthew's death. At Georgetown all classrooms have crucifixes mounted above the teacher's desk, a policy that led to heated debate in the campus papers. The students listen to a Jewish lesbian define an American crucifixion.

At home, I watch more "Ellen" reruns on Lifetime TV, my standard after-school treat this fall, except now I'm marveling that twenty-four hours before I was standing right next to Ellen, and of course now I'm watching more of the coming-out episodes from the historic last season of her show. Suddenly the phone rings: it's Henry, my beloved creative writing teacher from high school. His letter about Matthew's death was published in the Durham *Morning Herald*. He is crying, explaining that he still knows so very little about gay issues. I realize he is coming to *me* for solace and approval; as a straight man who has devoted his life to the progressive education of children, he's now becoming a GLSEN (Gay, Lesbian, Straight Education Network) activist as well. I tell him I've just mailed a pile of materials to his students. All night long, my phone rings as other friends, gay and straight, check in with me. And when the phone isn't ringing I watch the gay history documentary "Out of the Past" on PBS. And I begin to shake all over.

Exhaustion, emotion, excitement, stress, grief, lack of sleep, political renewal, all of the above. I recount the many images from last night at the vigil: standing next to the eminent Frank Kameny. Watching transgender activist Jessica Xavier standing on a wall. All the lesbians and gay men who brought their dogs to the vigil. Some speaker asking us to bow our heads in silence and church bells tolling JUST AT THAT MOMENT and ringing eight, as though this was Matthew's voice at last. Stars above, the Capitol windows like stained glass, someone blowing bubbles, someone smoking pot, dark circles under eyes.

Sleep.

October 16

I grade midterms sitting stone-like in front of hours of television news covering Matthew's funeral. I watch local news, "Nightline," "Larry King Live," "Nightline," ABC, NBC, CBS, CNN; the funeral, the Fred Phelps protest outside of it, vigils across the nation. Elizabeth Birch and Andrew Sullivan vs. Jerry Falwell and the head of the Southern Baptists, who declare that Christian conservatives *are the only ones who truly love homosexuals* because they seek so "save" us. I am nauseous, longing for Jesus to show up in the night and slap the evangelists in their smug, pompous, homophobic faces. Over and over, I fight off my own desire to commit violence, take revenge. I feel a special rage toward the murderers' complicit girlfriends. I ask myself complex mystical questions: suppose—like the Nebraskan neo-Nazi who made hate calls to some rabbi's answering machine and later became an activist for tolerance—suppose the Wyoming girls become penitent gay rights activists? Do I believe in redemption?

Henry calls and says, "There aren't TWO SIDES. The gaybashers are Satan's recruits." He's right: the "reverends" demonstrate absolutely no soul-searching or remorse, no call for moderation, just enhanced insistence upon surrendering to Jesus. Bad, bad Bible quoting. Debate, grief, horror, media. I have to admire Elizabeth Birch's calm in the face of insane posturing by televangelists. This is the hardest thing: to keep cool while taking on fascists.

I find it impossible to go out tonight for the opening of women's basketball season at the GWU gym. I can't party at a pep rally just now. If I left the house at all, it would be to go to a gay bar on my block to drink with other grieving homos. I am *this close* to leaving academia altogether and just joining some gay action organization.

October 17

I read Chastity Bono's book, *Family Outing*, as I sit on church steps waiting for a neighborhood memorial service. I am HUNGRY for the ingathering of a service, and the church is packed, the focus is on Matthew, and the very Episcopalian service is a gay-welcoming antidote to the homophobic preachers on TV last night. Radical to see a woman bishop up there, laying healing hands on gay guys. I'm wearing a t-shirt that says "Be All You Can Be: A Militant Homosexual."

Cathy Renna is in my pew; we head out to the Reel Affirmations gay and lesbian film festival. There, she gives a moving speech, and there's a reception with lots of Q and A time, all of us invited to discuss our feelings. Cathy, now media director of GLAAD, gives an up-to-the-minute analysis from reporters she met in Wyoming. We talk about class issues: does Matthew Shepard, as a victim, receive more sympathy and media coverage because he was a conventionally attractive, white victim? Cathy ties together the media's cancellation of Ellen's TV show and Ellen's appearance on the Capitol steps. This is a huddle of activists; everyone gets "Remember Matthew" buttons. I will wear the "Remember Matthew" pin on my college backpack for three years, through five countries: Israel, New Zealand, Iceland, England, Canada.

I walk to campus that night, Saturday night, and my lesbian students take me to the Hung Jury and buy me drinks. They toast me for being a "cool-ass teacher." Later I'll realize they're all underage, 18 and 19, drinking with fake IDs, but I don't dwell on all that now. The Hung Jury was *my* bar, *my* place, too, when I was younger, 23 and 24, and my students want to hear about what it was like in those "olden days." So I regale them with tales about the great night in 1985 when I danced right there with my friends Jeanette Buck and Maria Maggenti, who went on to direct award-winning independent lesbian films. I do feel old when some clueless kid asks if I'm Andrea's MOTHER. I dance with my students. Later, I'll frame the photo of this night.

October 18

The full week has passed. I have a day off, and know exactly what I need to do. I go see Toni Morrison's *Beloved* so I can finally have a good cry, for three long private hours in the dark.

Learning To Be In A Skin
Sarah B. Burghauser

❦

Before I learned the tricks of navigating the grain of my self, before I knew it was okay to let my skin act as eyes like they had my whole life, before I noticed that my body retains memory more than my mind, and before Anaïs Nin, who remains my longest literary love affair, entered my life, I learned to be Dr. Carbone. Yes, *be* her. Wear her clothes. Embody her strut. Talk fast and fiery and spit sentences from between my teeth.

Dr. Carbone, a post-punk critic for whom anything European was enormously hipper than anything American, thrashed her hands about as she spoke, made her way in a high-speed swagger through labyrinthine tracks of thought, always to come out the other side triumphant and making perfect sense.

It's a first love story, really. And as first queer infatuations sometimes go, I was not sure then if I wanted to *be* Dr. Carbone, or if what I really wanted was to sleep with her; she had the fearless tenacity I dreamed of pulling off, always striking the right chords, the right balance of rigidity and humor, charm and severity, biting critique and refreshing generosity. And as first love stories also go, there is heartbreak, which we never quite get over.

Working together in a variety of capacities throughout college made me feel close to her. She was my academic advisor, thesis advisor, faculty mentor for the Gay Straight Alliance and erotica reading group, both of which I started. We sat on committees together, and she was my professor. We'd sometimes share a cigarette after class. She'd ask me how I thought class went and I was ecstatic to know she wanted my opinion. I was her spy, her confidant, her little darling. However much access it was possible to have to Dr. C, I had it.

Our class, Literature and Sexuality, began with a conversation on obscenity. She said for this class to work, we have to be comfortable talking about sex, using and hearing "dirty words," and really thinking about what they mean. She wriggled out of her torn leather trench coat and flung it over her desk. Chalk in hand, boots thumping on the classroom carpet, she sauntered over to the blackboard and scrawled the word *fuck* in block letters.

"I'll just begin with 'fuck,'" she said, and the students tittered and shifted. "Someone throw out another." Dr. Carbone adjusted the black plastic framed glasses on her nose and beckoned with her hand for more words.

There was silence and downcast eyes.

She flicked her fingers back and forth to coax out those words, which quivered on the tips of all our tongues, and accidentally hurled her scrap of chalk across the room, marking the opposite wall. And where there was silence and fear there now was rollicking laughter and we all slacked our tight shoulders and took deep, quenching breaths.

Dr. C took up space like no other woman I knew. She made her body as big as possible, gesticulating and traipsing about as if appraising her surroundings.

"Well, how about this," she said, and took another piece of chalk and scribbled underneath *fuck*, the word *motherfucker*. "We can have the whole fuck family!" she cawed and scratched out *fucker*, *fuckwad*, and *fuckhead*.

Dr. C waxed analytical, trying to draw out of the students possible reasons why the word *motherfucker* might be considered an insult and then insisted students begin shouting out their favorite obscenities.

And it became Bacchanalian with the kind of unexpected pleasure students took while calling out, in full volume, the words *cocksucker*, *bitch*, *cunt*, *asshole*, *douche bag*, *shit head*, *pussy*, and so forth. The class was giddy, intoxicated by the permission to revel in the forbidden: language, which we knew existed and could express an incredible range of emotion and thought, but were not supposed to utilize. "I love all words!" she declared, at the height of our enjoyment.

Breathless after class, having just run a mental marathon to keep up with Carbone's New York style pop-culture sermonizing, I manifested her swagger in my hips, her march in my step. I attempted the composite of her badass attitude and disheveled, starved intellectual demeanor. I had studied her movements and knew them well. I liked how it felt to have her inhabit my frame and dictate my stride.

In the following weeks, we arranged ourselves in a circle. Tiny flip desks hovered over our laps. Our elbows almost touched in the circle, so packed there were no breaks in the corporeal connection, each body a physical witness to the energy flanking it.

Carbone would come in and, like every class, flop her leather coat on her desk and huff at some kink in her day, some minor frustration. We laughed, elated from the excitement of having ideas and from the thrill of watching and listening to Dr. C elucidate hers.

She dashed off diagrams of binaries, social structures and story plots on the blackboard. She slung more chalk, students scurried to pick it up for her – sweet and eager runners to do her bidding without even being asked. Once she flung her chalk and I got to it first. I rushed to replace it in her hand. I inched up to her, slouched near her side, careful not to get too close for fear I'd be in her way or perhaps that she would accidentally smack me with her unruly hand. I held the chalk out to her. But she didn't take it or even slow her speech or flash her eyes in my direction. Carbone continued her lecture. After holding my hand out for what felt like several minutes, I placed the chalk on the desk next to her coat and, tail between my legs, took my seat. Instead of studying her sentences and movements, I spent the remainder of that class watching the chalk waiting there for her.

Dr. Carbone had prided herself on being, what she called an "eat the cookie feminist": a woman who does not apologize for taking her pleasure, who thrives on excess and who refuses to skimp on the things she desires. A permissive feminism. A decadent feminism.

In my senior year when she was my thesis advisor, Carbone bought a new laptop as incentive for her to quit smoking, begin exercising, and go on a diet. She kept the pact with herself. She went cold-turkey, lost weight, her face cleared of blemishes, and she chewed gum constantly. But her personality changed with her new lifestyle. Where she was brash before, she became cruel. Where she was inquisitive before, she became skeptical. And where she was jokey before, she became sarcastic. In one conference Dr. C said I was writing too much in my own voice, which academic analysis required I stifle. "Remember this," she said. "You. Know. *Nothing*." Something turned in her. She became a brute and hissed wicked critique. Whatever I wrote or said was not up to snuff.

For weeks I returned from our meetings crying. My friends joked about anonymously leaving a pack of cigarettes and a donut in her mailbox.

She was late for our meeting. I sat on the floor outside her office pretending to read. But I listened to footsteps on the stone floor hallway echoing from downstairs. The quality of click or thump told me who it was. Dr. C's step rang, the thorn of her heels popping on the rock floor.

In her office, she rattled on, making sure I knew she had to run to another meeting in just a few minutes and that she was sorry but we had to make this one quick. I didn't sit down because of the rush, suspended between Carbone's monologue and theatric gestures, and the door she was verbally pushing me toward.

Backlit, Dr. C was swamped in sunlight from the window behind her desk. I squinted to make out her face, but I just saw a flock of single wiry hairs trying to flee her head. She flew through an assortment of topics: course material, her sister, winter break, my thesis, and the erotica reading group. I kept up, following every miniscule lull, every lilt, every beat of speech.

She sat at the lip of her seat. A poster from Eddie Izzard's show "Circle" was pinned to the wall above her head. It showed a fleshy deep purple flower unfurling so I could see its insides, a slow portal opening to new stratums of delicate skin, promising more layers beyond the visible page. If it were a real life flower, I thought it would siphon and swallow me. Dr. C talked and my gaze flashed between her flailing hands and the vampish flower. She flapped her arms and flicked her wrists, fingers stiff succulents on the bony trunks of her hands. A strange and gawky bird pollinating. The flower a witness.

"Try Anaïs Nin," I heard her say, and I jotted down the name.

Reading Nin made me realize that while Dr. Carbone was a mirror, reflecting back to me my own insecurities, Anaïs was something much more exquisite. Something much more complex. Anaïs was a prism that contained a whole spectrum of meaning, each of her words renewing my faith in the process of discovery, the process of learning, the process of seeing my self. And that these processes cannot be rushed. Anaïs' books became my cracked-open heart in front of me, all desires, all angst, all pain, all bliss splayed out and staring back. Dr. C gave me Anaïs, and Anaïs gave me back the self I had lost in my infatuation.

It occurs to me now that my love for Dr. Carbone had less to do with the ideas, theories, and stories she recounted in class, and more do with how she moved through space. I listened intently, of course, but I *watched*, too. Every flick of wrist, glint of eyes, thump of step was mine to examine, adopt, play with. I paid more and more attention to how specific bodies occupied space and the way my own body's shape affected what information I was able to absorb.

And then enter Anaïs who, amongst so many more revelations, taught me that a person's physical shape can embody an idea. Her writing, while deeply psychological and existential, always uses the body as a reference point, always returns to visceral details, sensation, the impression of desire on the way a person moves.

Intrigue about the body is the first curiosity we experience. We need to know how our limbs work, what it feels like to touch clothing of varying textures, the skin and smell of a parent, how to clutch our fingers around an object, and how to articulate what our bodies need.

In classrooms, we try to ignore the fact that we are not merely minds grappling with ideas and memories to make sense of the world. We ignore the heat of flesh, each beating heart asserting its rhythm, sometimes momentarily in sync, sometimes in complimentary opposition. And now, too, I see that this visceral learning is a queered process: one that involves all our human faculties, including corporeality, desire, and love. A radical learning, a defiant learning, a learning that unites the body and the mind.

I need a complete learning experience: one in which I can trace my histories with lovers, students, teachers, peers, chosen families, and friends. We impact each other with a multiplicity of techniques and with various qualities of touch: touches that are both spiritual and physical, maddening and grounding.

My queer mode of knowing is also erotic; it involves the transmission of love. Queers need to be literate in love, to teach with embodied desire, to connect with their context in order to be honest with themselves. The feeling of being in love is all-encompassing.

When we are in love, all our senses are heightened and we discover ourselves in brand new ways by allowing others into our space, into our bodies, into our minds.

Through the physicalization of learning I came into myself. I connected with untouched parts of me and came into a new community, a new history, a new story of who I could become. And when I lugged my bags of books from Dr. Carbone's office to the library, I found Anaïs, took her out, brought her back to my room, and fell in love again.

"Who Do I Have to Forgive to Move On From This Place?": *Meditations from a Third World Feminist Lesbian*
Kristie Soares

ᏭᎤ

My favorite quote from famed scholar/activist/healer Gloria Anzaldúa reads, "Some of us are leftists, some of us are practitioners of magic. Some of us are both" (*This Bridge* 209). Indeed, after years of Women's Studies coursework and a lifetime of enacting border identities, I have come to recognize that in any situation I am undeniably "both." I am both she and he, both the border crosser and the border guard, both the lawbreaker and the law itself. I began my journey as a Ph.D. student at a prestigious California university with this quote, and the concept of "both," fresh in my mind. After several years of being a nomad—living in Miami, Gainesville, Boulder, and back again—I had finally arrived in California. It was here that my partner and I had decided to settle. It was here that we were going to register to vote, plant flowers in our back yard, and finally paint the walls of our home. It was in California that I was going to finally become "myself," pin down this nomadic identity, and figure out who "I" was. It was here that I could finally stop living as "both" and be "one." Just "one."

The first quarter of my Ph.D. program, I enrolled in a seminar entitled Decolonizing Feminism, taught by none other than one of my idols—U.S. Third World Feminist scholar Chela Sandoval. What I did not know at the time was that this course would threaten my desire for a stable identity and bring me back, once again, to what Anzaldúa called a *nepantla* state—the condition of being between conditions, of being a bridge maker, of being always decidedly "both." It is from this *nepantla* state that I have learned to negotiate graduate school, and from which I write this meditation today. What follows is a compilation of academic and personal musings that chronicle how my experiences in a Decolonizing Feminism course helped me to survive my first year as a third world feminist lesbian in a Ph.D. program.

In college I was a revolutionary. I was a performance poet. I was an activist. I was everything that I have spent the rest of my twenties trying to recapture. Every time I performed poetry on stage with someone else, every show I helped organize, every feminist classroom I sat in, I was doing the difficult coalition work that I have since only read about in most graduate classrooms. It was a time when my identity was "at the edge of the skin," as I shared myself freely with those around me (Rowe 35). It was a time when sameness was not a prerequisite for holding the same social vision, and people came together.

Then I went to graduate school, where performing power is nine tenths of the game and coalition doesn't help you get ahead in the graduate classroom. It was a difficult transition that demanded I develop a consciousness to help me navigate my different performances of self. I had to develop an awareness that could witness all of the other versions of "me," which is what Anzaldúa calls "conocimiento." I had to find some way to avoid buying into the roles I was playing. As Anzaldúa says, "After years of wearing masks we may become just a series of roles, the constellated self limping along with its broken limbs" (*Making Face* xv). During the first year of my Ph.D. program I struggled to create a consciousness that kept me in touch with the interface between these masks.

When I arrived in California I was in the process of searching for new ways to deepen my *conocimiento*. I had become so proficient in the language of White male Eurocentric philosophy and could play the game so convincingly that I had become, I feared, one of "them." I was afraid that I had abandoned my roots and internalized everything I had intended to rebel against. What if graduate school had only pushed me further away from the spiritual being that I had been all along?

I was thinking about these issues when I read Cherríe Moraga's essay "Long Line of *Vendidas*." I wrote:

> I am so conflicted about Moraga's piece! I've read it many times before and recognize that it gives voice to thoughts I myself have had: "White lesbians don't get me"…"You couldn't pay me to go to the Michigan Womyn's

Festival"…"It's not cool to claim you're a lesbian if you don't sleep with women"… But at the same time all of these thoughts are ones I would later go on to question once I pushed myself to think critically. Although it's true that certain groups of feminists or lesbians don't feel welcoming to me, my antagonism toward them doesn't make it any better. So when Moraga makes sweeping statements about White women it drives me crazy because she's erecting boundaries between people, but at the same time she's echoing the little voice inside of me that thinks things like: 'Why did I sign up for a graduate class in the English department? These dry White people have no interest in talking about anything socially relevant.'

Indeed, my attempts at achieving a greater level of coalition building had often led me to the issues I expressed in this free write. Although on a spiritual level I felt a connection with all beings, it was often hard to witness this kinship in certain situations. Just as Moraga expressed disillusionment with the behavior of some white feminists, so too had I found myself frustrated with the behavior of certain colleagues since arriving at my Ph.D. program.

This power struggle became most apparent in the graduate classroom, which seemed to exist primarily as a space for graduate students to flaunt their knowledge. Each week I would grow more and more frustrated as my colleagues manipulated the conversation with talk about dead philosophers, rather than material realities. In one instance, during a class discussion about exile, important contributions about the conditions of political exile (poverty, feelings of displacement, etc.) were deflected by one student's diatribe on the meaning of the word "political." What had started as an open dialogue about the implications of political exile art, quickly deteriorated into this student's quest to define politics, from Aristotle onward. In this class, as in other academic settings, I often watched angrily as my colleagues lost themselves in the rhetorical and linguistic games of academic theory, in order to escape dealing with existing social inequalities — inequalities that affected my life as a lesbian, a Latina, and a human being.

Once again I found myself having to deal with the difficulties of doing *nepantlera* work. How can I create bridges between my world and the purely theoretical world of my colleagues? How can I avoid seeing them as the enemy? How can I learn to care about what they say, when they clearly have no interest in what I say? What happens if I don't form these coalitions? Will I find, as feminist scholar Maria Lugones does, that "the more independent I am, the more independent

I am left to be?" (7). Over and over again in this situation I forced myself to remember Moraga's words: "any movement built on the fear and loathing of anyone is a failed movement" (190). For me, the first year of my Ph.D. program was an exercise in working through this fear and loathing. It was a process of remembering that different skin color, sexual identity, and theoretical vocabulary are poor indicators of a person's truth.

Moving to California also brought up issues of cultural identity for me. I am, inescapably, a half-breed: half Cuban heritage and half Brazilian heritage, half American citizen and half ethnic Other, half here and half there. I grew up in a Latin American family, but I have spent my entire adult life living in primarily White towns interacting with primarily White folks. I would be lying if I didn't admit that I sometimes feel more at home outside of my hometown of Miami. Moving out West brought up many of these issues of cultural belonging that I thought I had dealt with years before. To my surprise, a move across the country will bring up skeletons you had long shoved in the back of the closet. You could say it swung the door of my closet wide open—so to speak.

I faced this cultural baggage during one session of our Decolonizing Feminism class. As part of a small group exercise I was asked: " What tools do you have to combat colonization?" I wrote:

> How do I combat colonization? I do it by being smarter than the colonizer, because I can never change the way I look but I can change how much I know. So it's true I often have slip ups in any of the languages I speak... My Spanish vocabulary never seems to be large enough to express my opinions in Spanish graduate seminars. A slip of the tongue usually gives me away as a second-generation Brazilian when speaking Portuguese. Even my English has felt limited, with several botched idioms when trying to communicate with my American office mates. But at least I speak 3 more languages than most people in power. It's true that I didn't go to private school, but do you have a PhD? It's true that I'm brown and a lesbian, but when I'm a professor and your kid is in my class I have the power to teach him anything I want.

In this free write I echoed many of the cultural issues that I had faced since moving to California: issues of feeling like the only brown person in a primarily white town, issues of having to use my high level of education as a first line of defense against prejudice, issues of always feeling out of place in my native languages. The most difficult part of the situation, however, was feeling left out even amongst those that shared my culture. As the only out lesbian in my Ph.D. program, I often found that other Latinas misunderstood my experiences as much as my White colleagues did.

I received a lesson in looking past these differences during one session of Decolonizing Feminism. In a discussion about gender roles, one female Latina student shared: "When my husband gets home at 7:00 I feel compelled to start cooking and cleaning. I don't know why. He doesn't ask me to, but when he's home it just feels right, in a way it doesn't when he's not home." I was shocked to hear this student share these feelings, because—much to my surprise—I could relate. I later wrote:

> Girl I feel you. But not in the way you think. I'm not going to pretend I've done a large amount of research on what it'd be like to be a heterosexual female, but I can say that in all my years of dating men I never felt so entrenched in a female role as I do in my lesbian relationship now. My girlfriend and I are both what you might call "femme" lesbians (a term that can barely begin to get at the various ways one can be both a woman and a lesbian). But yet even with her long hair and occasional skirt wearing, something about her still makes me feel like I should be grabbing a dishrag.

In this free write I meditated on the unexpected similarities between myself—a queer graduate student in a long-term relationship—and my classmate—a heterosexual, married undergraduate. I was surprised to find that I felt oppressed by gender roles in a way that was similar to my classmate. How could I have missed such an obvious connection? I asked myself. Why would I assume that I have nothing in common with this classmate, just because she was straight and an undergraduate? How many other similarities must there be between myself and my other classmates?

This free write served as a way for me to come to terms with my own tendency to see differences between myself and others. It was a concrete reminder of the work that I must continue to do to "decolonize" myself, and to be able to build coalitions. It showed me that being intellectually committed to third world feminism is not enough. One must do the inner work that the third world feminists advocate, in order to be the kind of person that can truly articulate a third world feminist coalitional politics.

The turning point in the first year of my Ph.D. program came during one session of my Decolonizing Feminism course after reading the words of third world feminist scholar M. Jacqui Alexander. Alexander writes about the process of coalition building, stating that it is a daily practice requiring: "revolutionary patience, courage, and above all humility" (101). Reading this statement caused a shift in my consciousness. If only I could learn to have the patience and bravery necessary to be humble (a quality not generally prized in graduate school), I realized I would be able to make deeper connections with others. If only I could forgive my colleagues for seeing me as other, I could stop othering them as well. If only I could move past the boundaries between myself and others, I would realize there are no boundaries between myself and others. After the reading the article, I wrote the following:

> This article is literally changing my life...it offers a way to do the activist work I've been called to do in academia but feed my soul at the same time... but at the same time it's scary because making coalition with people on this profound level—not just to get what you want, but to heal and decolonize yourself—is very scary. It requires accepting who you are and revealing it to other people...it requires forgiving them for staring at me when I walk down the street holding hands with my partner. It's difficult, but I'm ready to heal. Who do I have to forgive to move on from this place?

To me this free write represents the definitive point in my journey toward *conocimiento*, or awareness. At the moment when I wrote these words, I opened myself up to a witnessing consciousness that was able to observe me as I observed these feelings. The moment was so profound that within days I found I had been transformed. It was as though my question, "Who do I have to forgive to move on from this place?" was instantly answered.

By tapping into this consciousness I came to realize over the next several days that my experiences over the past few months did not represent the totality of my being. During these months I had been erecting barriers between others and myself for survival in my Ph.D. program. Although I did not recognize it at the time, they were modes of resistance that I had employed to survive. For me, witnessing a level of consciousness in which I could dis-identify with these tropes marked a definitive point in my *conocimiento*. It allowed me to see myself as more than just the sum of my actions, thought patterns, and identity categories. It pushed me to see myself as I had before becoming a graduate student—as a spiritual being doing profoundly spiritual work in an academic setting. This confirmation of my nature has influenced my interactions with others, my coalition building, and my feminist politics. It has brought me again to the *nepantlera* state from where I write this meditation on being a third world feminist lesbian in academia today.

Works Cited

Alexander, M. Jacqui. "Remembering *This Bridge*, Remembering Ourselves: Yearning, Memory, and Desire." *This Bridge We Call Home: Radical Visions for Transformation*, Eds. Gloria E. Anzaldúa and AnaLouise Keating. New York: Routledge, 2002.

Anzaldúa, Gloria. *Making Face, Making Soul/Haciendo Caras: Creative and Critical Perspectives by Women of Color*. San Francisco: Aunt Lute, 1990.

Anzaldúa, Gloria. *This Bridge Called My Back: Writings by Radical Women of Color*. San Francisco: Aunt Lute Press, 1981.

Carrillo Rowe, Aimee. *Power Lines: On the Subject of Feminist Alliances*. Durham: Duke, 2008.

Lugones, María. "Playfulness, 'World'-Traveling, and Loving Perception." *Hypatia* 2.2, Summer 1987, 7.

Moraga, Cherríe. *Loving in the War Years*. Cambridge: South End, 1983.

Transitions
Lori Horvitz

❧

During a discussion about the death penalty, Katie, a student in my composition class, opened a bag of Doritos and munched away. I tried to ignore her chewing and bag crackling, but soon enough I could no longer contain my anger. "This is not a cafeteria!" I said. "Put those away!"

Besides the background ventilation system blowing cold air from the ceiling, the room was silent. Katie sat up, glared at me and closed her bag.

Katie, a freckled-faced tomboy, arrived late on a regular basis, and after plopping herself down, she'd flip through a newspaper or read a book. When asked to participate in discussions, she'd sigh, reluctantly close her newspaper or book and stare straight ahead.

By the second week of the semester, I dreaded walking into the room.

The day the Twin Towers crumbled to the ground, Katie slumped in her desk. She said, "We deserve it. We think we're so safe. Our country is run by a bunch of assholes."

Other students shook their heads, wept, talked of relatives or friends who knew one of the victims. For the first time, students thought about war and body bags and military drafts.

Katie crossed her arms. "This is a wake-up call," she said, "to Bush and his stupid-ass cabinet." She kept at it. But now, at least, her aggression wasn't directed towards me.

One day I asked to speak with her after class. "You're obviously smart," I said, "but you seem to have an attitude problem."

Katie sat at a desk, looked at the ground and jiggled her leg. "I shouldn't be in school. I hate all of my classes." She fingered a fresh bruise, one of many, on her arm.

"Were you in an accident?" I asked.

"They're from the Fight Club," she said.

Based on the movie, Katie started the club for girls on campus, an exclusive group that took on new members by invitation only. On a weekly basis they'd get together, and two at a time, beat the crap out of each other. Katie mentioned that two other students in my class, Rachel and Cindy—girly-girls who dressed in skirts and heels, were also members of the club.

The idea of a women's fight club sounded subversive, edgy, maybe even feminist. I imagined the young women hopping around each other, swinging arms and fists, hands blocking faces, one woman pinning another's arms to the ground, a group on the sidelines cheering.

I wanted to know more. Before I could rifle off questions, she said, "I've already told you too much. First rule of the Fight Club is not to talk about the Fight Club." From her binder, she pulled a graded paper, asked why I gave her a B on it.

I looked it over, said, "First off, you moved from one topic to the next without using transitions."

"I don't believe in transitions," she said.

"But you need transitions!"

"Why?"

"I'm all for experimenting with language," I said, "but you've got to show me you know the rules before you break them."

Katie, the valedictorian of her high school class, told me she'd always gotten A's on her papers. "The only thing that's keeping me here," she said, "is the Fight Club." She looked at her arms again. "And with the financial aid I'm getting, I can't afford *not* to be in school."

"Perhaps you could write about the Fight Club," I said, "for your next paper."

Katie shook her head. "No way. It's a private matter," she said, and stormed out of the classroom.

In my freshman year of college, Tami, a tai-chi expert who lived on my hall, showed women how to spar, how to strengthen our stance, how we needed to use footwork or faking to bring our partner closer to us, how to pin our opponent down if the opportunity arose. The stoned hippie boys who lived at the end of the hall watched us get sweaty, laugh, fall atop each other.

Three years later, I began a romance with one of the hippie boys. After our first kiss, he said, "I always thought you were a lesbian."

"Why'd you think that?"

"You seemed to really like sparring," he said, "with women."

"Men wrestle all the time!" I said.

We continued to kiss.

I went to a college where same-sex couples walked hand-in-hand, where the gay and lesbian union was the most popular group on campus. During my first week there, I met another student, Eric, from my hometown. Both of us had been loners, outcasts in high school. Now he was a flaming queer. "This is a great place to be gay," he said.

When I told my mother about Eric, she said, "He's probably just pretending to be gay."

But me, I was straight. Except one day in my dorm-room when I listened to Fleetwood Mac's *Rumours* over and over again while staring at the back cover of the album, at Stevie Nicks in her silk gown. I felt a pang of lust, attraction. I felt dirty. Freakish. I lifted the phonograph's arm and switched records. I put on Bob Segar's *Nightmoves*. And I sat on my bed, rocking back and forth, saying to myself, "I'm not like that. I'm not like that."

To prove I was desirable, that I wasn't like "that," I drank and drank and drank and made out with boys, some of whom I didn't even like. Isn't that what girls were supposed to do?

The semester Katie tormented me, I was getting over a relationship with a woman who I feared because of her guns and temper. For the first time in nine years, I attempted to date men. One night, Katie walked by an outdoor café, saw me with one of my dates. "Hi Dr. Horvitz," she said, sniggering to her friend, as if catching me in a lie.

At the time, I convinced myself that women were too damn difficult; I needed to get married, have a baby and live a "normal" life. Fortunately, after one of my dates leaned over to kiss me in his tiny Toyota, I snapped out of *that* thought bubble.

During my first year of teaching composition, I lived in a Manhattan tenement flat, a sixth-floor walk-up. From my back window, I could see the Twin Towers, two shiny invincible rectangles hovering above lower Manhattan. Back then, we were fearful, not of terrorists, but of AIDS. In class, my students read and discussed *The Normal Heart*, a play that addresses love, homophobia and the AIDS epidemic in its first years.

Some students questioned why people were gay in the first place. One said, "It's *not* normal!" Others said they had relatives who were gay, that they were nice people, but they didn't want to see them expressing themselves in public. Another student, a Russian immigrant, shook her head and said, "It's their business what they do in the bed!" When I asked how they'd feel if they knew one of their teachers were gay or lesbian, one female student raised her hand and said, "I'd feel weird when she looked at me."

President Bush told us to shop, Wal-Mart sold out of American flags and Katie continued to undermine my authority. She tapped her fingers on her desk, grunted answers out when called upon, and sometimes fell asleep. Towards the end of the semester, students spoke about their upcoming paper topics—I asked them to write about a current news event from a sociological perspective. Katie planned to write about a Brazilian tribe in the Amazon rainforest that was known for walking around in the nude, from the point of view of 18th century philosopher Thomas Aquinas.

"But that's not a current event," one of the students said.

"They're still walking around in the nude, so they're current," Katie said.

No matter how much I talked to Katie outside of class, no matter how much I acted like I was in control, inside I was falling apart. Similar to a romantic relationship, once you feel broken down, once you show your vulnerabilities, it's hard to regain composure, unless, as far as a romance goes, you walk away. But when you're teaching college, you can't walk away. You're stuck for a full fifteen weeks.

After all, I'm just as vulnerable as the next person. I cry at the movies. Dumb movies. Smart movies. I can't hold back. I tell myself, *Stop crying! It's just a stupid movie! Hugh Grant would never get together with his plant-sitter.* But I can't stop. I even cry when I hear the piña colada song.

So how could I *not* get upset when I read Katie's comments about the class? Teacher evaluations are anonymous, but I knew it was Katie who wrote: *I wanted to be a writer but she totally discouraged me. She took my confidence away. Now I no longer want to be a writer. I hate her.*

I questioned myself, my teaching.

Soon after the class ended, a university staff person found bloodstains on the floor of a room the group had secretly met in. The Fight Club disbanded. Katie dropped out of school.

Two years later, Katie reappeared in my poetry class, sitting in the back of the room. As if an ex-lover came back to haunt me, I wanted to run. Although she took notes and barely looked up, I stuttered when calling out names, when going over the syllabus.

But this time around, Katie behaved, made intelligent comments, wrote A papers. Mid-way through the semester, she stepped into my office, her eyes to the ground. She asked if I could talk with her about her mid-term paper. "Have a seat," I said.

Even though we didn't acknowledge our past, its presence made itself known, like a boulder in the corner of a dream.

Together we brainstormed; she scribbled in her notebook, asked questions, and while still looking at the floor, thanked me for my time.

"I hope I was helpful," I said.

She nodded her head, cowered away.

The next year, she was in another class of mine, a writing workshop. Once again her performance was stellar. During a one-on-one conference, I looked over a draft of her personal essay—a coming out story.

"It's powerful," I said, "without being sentimental. And you use transitions well."

She furled her brow, said, "Really?"

In her last semester, Katie asked me to be her thesis advisor.

Just before graduation, during a concert intermission, Katie strolled up to me and acted as if we'd been long lost friends. "Hey, Lori," she said. "How's it going?" She introduced me to her girlfriend. I introduced her to my girlfriend. "This is Katie," I said. "She's a student of mine, a great writer. But when she was in my comp class, she was *such* an asshole!"

Katie scowled, shut her eyes, shook her head. "I figured you'd forgotten about that."

"How could I forget?"

"I was drinking too much," she said, "and doing drugs. I *was* an asshole. I'm sorry." The musicians came back on stage and the crowd cheered.

We returned to our seats.

Soon after, she attended a literary reading I participated in. Now she was my groupie in the front row.

Two years later, Katie e-mailed me with a request for a graduate school recommendation. I told her I'd be happy to write one. In a postscript, I asked about the Fight Club.

This time, in an e-mail, she obliged:

The whole thing was very sexually charged, which I wouldn't have admitted at the time. I think it partially arose from all of these mutual and bizarre crushes my friends had on each other. I remember being in a dorm room with Rachel and another freshman and they were talking about what they called 'girl crushes.' I had this realization then that lesbians weren't all stereotypes and could actually be attractive and fashionable and human! And that sort of changed my life. The fight club was like making out with our fists.

We used to drink 40s of Highlife and sneak into this room no one ever used that had industrial carpet and this bizarre Inferno theme and beat the shit out of each other (although, admittedly, most of our wounds came from rug burn when this 200 pound girl rubbed our faces in the carpet). It was pretty clear who was good and who wasn't. I think we used to stick to sort of informal and unspoken classifications. Rachel and I were both well-matched and two of the better fighters. Seems like neither one of us was willing to admit defeat so our fights would go on forever and end when everyone else got sick of watching us. We tried to leave it all in the room, you know—to get over any ego or disappointments and hug each other when it was over.

I feel lucky to have met all of those girls when it felt like everyone around us was trying to fit into the imaginary "college girl" mold. That year was filled with drunken mischief. At the end of the year about two dozen of us, boys and girls, played naked soccer on the quad in the middle of the night and walked back in the dorm barefoot, dirty, and completely undressed. Too bad everyone had to grow up.

After I sent out the recommendation, she sent me an e-mail:

Thanks again for your help. My eighteen-year-old self would never have believed that I would want your recommendation six years later.

I think about my eighteen-year-old self, drunk and slurry on white Russians, making out with boys or, sweaty and giddy, sparring with women on my dorm-room floor. At the time, I'd never believe I'd become a college professor, wrestling, metaphorically, with students, teaching about the need for transitions, all the while, stumbling upon a few of my own.

Thank heavens we all grow up.

Dr. 'Strange'love Or How I Learned to Stop Worrying and Start Loving (in) the Classroom Closet[1]

Jules Odendaul-James

ℭℑ

I would be lying if I said I wasn't angry. Despite the rhetoric found in various conservative activist quarters about the homosexualization of the ivory tower, there is little being done to afford basic recognition and protection for actual homosexuals who work and study at many public universities. For instance, while there may be in an increase in queer-identified graduate students who also serve their departments as instructors and teaching assistants, suspicion and hostility are also on the rise across campuses—from faculty, administration, and other graduate and undergraduate students. An instructor who includes a unit or even a single reading addressing anything queer—such as an article that acknowledges that queer people exist – can receive student evaluations with comments that range from the more innocuous—"Too many lesbians," (as if that's possible!)—to the more extreme, "This course indoctrinates students into homosexuality" (like *that* would ever get past the curriculum committee).

The university from which I received my doctorate and where, during my tenure as a graduate student, I often taught a 2-2 load, has said it does not discriminate on the basis of sexual orientation. Even in 2010, however, this is a proclamation without teeth. I wonder now, as I did when I was a graduate student, why does this lip-service approach to same-sex equality persist here even as other equally "red" states' public universities offer domestic partner benefits to their queer faculty and staff?[2] Since there are few public discussions of such policies, I offer only the rumors I heard during my tenure. That the administration is afraid of alienating federal government and ROTC programs which remain empowered in discrimination by the Clinton-era dual legacies of "Don't Ask, Don't Tell" and the Defense of Marriage Act. That the legislature, not to mention, the people of this great southern state are a conservative crowd still suspicious of the very notion of "liberal arts." Thus, the sixteen campuses articulate a policy on nondiscrimination that amounts to the words "sexual orientation" being penciled in among a laundry list of other "differences." To be fair, this university system also claims not to discriminate against individuals with physical disabilities, but in multiple campuses across the state, it neglects to put ramps to and elevators in the buildings[3]—ostensibly because they're landmarks, they're historic, they're part of traditions that include good ol' boys, public lynchings, and, yes, widespread homophobia.

I would be lying if I said I wasn't angry. But I am committed to improving our lot. In the face of these empty gestures, there are many tactics that one might pursue. Militancy that is out, loud, and proud. Diplomacy, out, proud, but not so loud. Or invisibility, because silence is golden and survival is an uphill battle. Some of us have employed more than one of these tactics—all of these tactics, even—in any given day. As a result, we find ourselves contributing to this anthology to share our experiences. Unfortunately, none of these tactics—militancy, diplomacy, invisibility—brings lasting happiness. And so I am here to offer *my* solution, one queer's response to this dilemma and to the ongoing negligence perpetrated by higher education administrations across the country. I call it: **militant invisibility**.

Militant invisibility is, first and foremost, a refusal to be an example. I am not a poster child. I am not a target. I speak my mind, but only among friends. I go to Pride Parades, wearing friendly slogan rainbow t-shirt with a bag over my head. Further, I am not knowable in the classroom. I don't offer myself up. I speak in hypotheticals, I watch my students from the sidelines—and some of them feel it. They are spurred to action, to ask, yet I do not divulge. I make them beg for it. If I'm going to be in the closet, I'm dragging them in with me. Eventually students stop self-disclosing, stop participating, even stop showing up. And you know as I do, that it is a heck of a lot easier to grade students when they never come to class. Or at least it's easier to grade papers that don't recount the myriad ways that it is a student's right (be it given by God or the Constitution) to refuse any arguments in support of civil rights for homosexuals. As one student asserted in a final writing assignment for a Social Theory and Cultural Diversity course I taught: "Because of judicial activism, two women might be allowed to create a relationship together but eventually Nature intercedes and one of them takes the role of 'The Man.' This is proof that lesbianism is inherently unnatural; God's law of Man and Woman will ultimately prevail." I was up most of the night trying to carefully craft a response that both deconstructed this argument and yet assured myself that the student wouldn't run to his Congressman to accuse me of bias.[4] In the end the student got a "B-" and I got a little bit smaller in my own eyes.

Now, I want to be very clear about this—militant invisibility is a choice. I made this choice as a graduate student instructor in order to deal with my environment. And it's all about choice—which is to say it's not about choice at all, but about the perception of choice as a political hot button issue. You have a choice to make the choice that was made for you. Please take a moment to marvel at the convenience of pre-chosen choices. Some may find it a tad presumptuous on the part of American society to foreclose on our potential as human beings to reach the fullness of experience, but we might also consider it a real time saver. With all the time I have on my hands, I decorate my closet. This plumage is another tool of militant invisibility: being flamboyantly "in." Women—wear lots of silver jewelry and vests, but explain it away by saying you're from Arizona. Men—when you show up to work looking very natty, tell folks you got a visit from the Queer Eye guys or have been transformed by those Dove for Men commercials.

I know these suggestions sound like I'm advocating that you lie, that you suppress who you are. I know, I know: silence = death; I am who I am; to thine own self be true. But face it—aren't you tired of the constant awareness? I'm saying we can make a choice to be exactly who they want us to be—so long as we do it with gusto. It's not the choice for everyone. And it is a choice; the way elections are a choice. By that I mean you can tell it's rigged even when your candidate wins. In any event, straight people make choices all the time, so why can't we? They can choose to look gay. They can choose to write about their queerness, even if that lifestyle amounts to more style than life. I don't want to argue that you don't know gay until you are gay. All I know is that it is easier to be gay when you're straight—so why shouldn't it be easier to be straight when you're gay?

Try this exercise: keep a journal and everyday write in it about your experiences as a heterosexual—went to farmer's market, did laundry, filed joint income tax form. Fairly straightforward, so to speak. Next, start saving for that wedding, enjoy that promotion at work, enjoy a well-funded retirement that protects your survivors after your death. Heterosexuality is the blank canvas and you are Norman Rockwell. Heterosexuality is the new black, which was the new white, which used to be off-white until someone on TLC's *What Not To Wear* decided that it was okay to wear white after Labor Day. This is the second phase of militant invisibility—perform heterosexuality, but perform it poorly. That's right—ladies, marry the guy, but don't take his name and be sure to wear only pants. And gents, host the Superbowl party but serve delicious, low calorie hors d'oeuvres in a French maid's outfit. Now it is resoundingly simplistic to equate gender identification with sexual preference. It is a gross oversimplification of the human psyche and desire. But everyone from Oprah to CNN does it, so why not me?

I told you—I'm angry, but thanks to a prolonged graduate education, I can cite several scholars who support my point of view. For now, I'll just give an extended quote from one: Alice Dreger, Professor of Clinical Medical Humanities and Bioethics at the Feinberg School of Medicine at Northwestern University.[5] Dreger has been a guest on Oprah and writes a blog for *Psychology Today*; she studies and councils patients, doctors, and families around issues dealing with medical interventions on non-normative bodies, particularly intersexed individuals who exemplify the tangled web among sex, gender, sexual desire, appearance, and function. In a 1998 *New York Times* editorial, Dreger encouraged parents and medical professionals to change their mindsets instead of changing their children's/patient's bodies: "...just because it makes sense that you ought to be able to fix anatomically based psychosocial problems anatomically, that doesn't mean it is so. Working to eliminate social stereotypes would be more effective and better for everyone in the long run."[6] Her meticulous research and public advocacy is a gift to those of us who strive to complicate the notion that sex organs, gender performances, and sexual desires do or should have "natural" or inherent connections.

Okay, I've been ignoring the obvious—that many of us are already performing heterosexuality very badly. I mean if you're supposed to be a heterosexual, having sex with someone of the *same* sex is a serious slip off the straight and narrow. (Unless you're on Bravo's *Real Housewives of Who Gives a Damn*.) Granted, it's a lot of fun, but it's not standard operating procedure. And it's worse if you have sex with people of the same sex, people of the opposite sex, and maybe even people of indeterminate sex, and maybe even puppets. Clearly you can make a choice. You can make a choice the way you chose to go to graduate school – I mean, it seemed like a good idea at the time, right? Or you didn't know what else to do after you received your bachelor's degree. Or the job market soured. Or maybe you went graduate school on purpose, to learn for learning's sake— stranger things have happened. Whatever the reason, militant invisibility can help you the way it has helped me. Just remember these key points: if you're going to be in the closet, be loud about it, and, if that fails, perform heterosexuality but do it badly. For the latter, I recommend having sex with your partner, significant other, or honeybuns (whichever euphemism you prefer) right there on the copy machine in the departmental lounge. Now that's being a bad straight person.

Of course, I'm still angry. I'm angry because militant invisibility has little to no hope of making academic life better—although it is fun to wait until one of your students, colleagues, or professors gets to the end of a gay joke before you say, "Speaking of dildos, my girlfriend and I... " That's amusing, but it's not as enjoyable as being sure I wouldn't be fired for being visibly, vocally gay in the classroom. Or that I would be hired despite being visibly, vocally gay. Surely, I think, it can't be that big a request. Then I remember what the former chancellor of my university said at the first public "hooding" ceremony for doctoral students. Wearing colored regalia that signified his degree in fine arts, he smirked as he told the audience not to "read anything into" the **pink** on his robe. This comment spurred some outraged discussion on the progressive faculty email list, but no one, not a single student or faculty, took the chancellor to task publicly. That's militant invisibility at its finest. Of course, we can do better, but we need help. We need real nondiscrimination policies. We need administrators who aren't afraid of pink. We need to do something so that we're not so angry all the time. It would be a start.

Postscript

I would be lying if I said things have not gotten better. Even though in 2004 constitutional amendments prohibiting "same-sex marriage" or any civil equivalent of marriage for same-sex couples passed in eight US states, in 2005 same-sex civil marriage rights bills become law in Canada, Spain and the United Kingdom. By 2010, American same-sex couples can be married or enjoy civil partnerships with the corresponding (state) rights of marriage in Iowa, Massachusetts, Connecticut, Vermont, New Hampshire, and the District of Columbia.

While there was a set-back to marriage equality with the 2008 passage of California's Proposition 8, and Maine's Proposition 1, in the summer of 2010, federal judges in California rule that both Proposition 8 and the U.S. Armed Forces' policy regarding gay service members are unconstitutional measures specifically designed to limit the free speech, freedom of expression and rights to equal protection and due process under the law for queer Americans. These legal opinions place increasing pressure on the administration of President Barack Obama to dismantle the Defense of Marriage Act and "Don't Ask, Don't Tell."

I should be happy, right? I mean after almost a decade of wrangling, in October 2009 Congress passed and President Obama signed the Matthew Shepard and James Byrd Jr. Hate Crime Prevention Act that specifically expands the federal hate-crimes law to include crimes motivated by a victim's "actual or perceived gender, sexual orientation, gender identity, or disability." Of course, the Employment Non-Discrimination Act languishes in committee again precisely because it designates sexual orientation and gender identity as non-discriminatory categories. In April of 2010, President Obama instructed Kathleen Sebelius, the Secretary of Health and Human Services, to inform all hospitals that participate in Medicare and Medicaid that they cannot deny visitation privileges on the basis of "sexual orientation" or "gender identity." But this is a largely symbolic gesture since provisions requiring insurers and employers to cover domestic partners are left out of the 2010 Health Care Reform Bill.

I'm still angry because, as these last few significant policy changes indicate, the "rights" that queer Americans have secured (or are close to securing) are the right to be killed in military actions, the right to have our murders prosecuted with extra vigor, and the right to watch a loved one die. Militant invisibility at its most dishearteningly literal. I still hope that we might, as Alice Dreger suggests, continue to change minds instead of ourselves in order to live peacefully, prosperously, and publicly. Some of us already are. It's a start.

Notes

1. This piece was originally presented at the November 2004 National Communication Association annual conference in Chicago, IL as part of a roundtable on being a queer teaching assistant/using queer material in the classroom, sponsored by the Caucus on Gay and Lesbian Concerns. I must thank my partner Kelly Rowett-James for her invaluable feedback on this and many other pieces.

2. According to an April 2010 report compiled by Alene Russell, Senior State Policy Consultant for the American Association of State Colleges and Universities, "red" state, public Research Universities that provide benefits for same-sex domestic partners include the University of Montana, the University of Utah, Florida State University, the University of Alabama at Birmingham, even the Universities of Alaska at Fairbanks and Anchorage.

3. Up until 2007 the Office of Disability Services at my doctoral institution's campus was located in a building where only the basement floor was wheelchair accessible.

4. Such a turn of events happened at my doctoral institution in the early spring of 2004. In a "Literature and Cultural Diversity" course, an adjunct instructor dealt with what she felt was hate speech by writing to the class listserv reiterating the rules of classroom debate. In this message, she identified a specific student, who framed his critique of homosexuality by his religious beliefs, as someone who spoke from a position of "white, heterosexual, Christian male" privilege. The student argued that the instructor was using those labels to silence him and to foment unwarranted hate against him, his beliefs, and his right to articulate those beliefs in the classroom. Another student forwarded the listserv exchange to the campus newspaper, which decried the situation as an example of conservative student suppression on campus. The story was picked up by local media and the student became a bit of a cause célébre, giving an interview about the incident to a local conservative talk show host whose broadcast caught the attention of a member of state's congressional delegation. The representative helped the student pursue his complaint of discrimination to the Office of Civil Rights (OCR) within the US Department of Health & Human Services. Incidentally, that office's nondiscrimination clause does not include discrimination on the basis of sexual orientation. (The adjunct faculty member in question is an out lesbian). While the instructor had her teaching contract renewed, she was deluged with hate mail and assigned a faculty observer who supervised her classroom for the rest of the semester. That same spring the Faculty Council approved a resolution on intellectual integrity and independence that ostensibly reinforced the university's anti-discrimination policy and preserved students' free speech and expression; however, the reaffirmation, framed by the OCR investigation, seemed to reinforce conservative activists' vocal critiques of the campus' progressive faculty. In September 2004, the OCR ruled that the instructor had violated the student's civil rights but the University was not required, nor did it seek, to pursue further action against her. The John William Pope Center offers its take on the events at http://www.popecenter.org/issues/article.html?id=1393. The university's LAMDA newsletter addresses the issue of administrative inaction on behalf of queer students and faculty in its article at http://www.unc.edu/glbtsa/lambda/articles/27/2/homophobia.htm. The local independent newspaper discusses the events in an article by Barbara Solow titled "Academia Under Siege" at http://www.indyweek.com/indyweek/academia-under-siege/Content?oid=1191788.

5. Dreger's homepage can be found at http://www.alicedreger.com/home.html.

6. "When Medicine Goes Too Far In the Pursuit of Normality." *New York Times Online*. 28 July 1998. http://www.nytimes.com/library/national/science/072898sci-essay.html.

Toward a Practice of Humility
By Mara Hughes

☙

Until June of 2010, I was a high school English teacher at a magnet
school in one of New Jersey's mid-sized post-industrial cities. There's
only one proper grocery store. Medical care is inconsistent enough
that three of my twelfth grade students developed pneumonia in
my first year of teaching in the district, and sometimes students
missed class for court appointments or long days at the WIC office.
The kids are brilliant, though, and the school is safe and friendly,
an environment any parent in America would be lucky to send her
child to each day.

I live in the city with my partner. I am a library cardholder, a
produce coop member, and a Pride Coalition staffer. I love it. It's
my chosen city, which means that I, unlike many of my neighbors,
have the means and opportunity to live somewhere else. It's a
scrappy town that's undergoing a number of exciting changes at
the grassroots level, and I'm incredibly proud to be a part of it.
Besides, our gorgeous loft apartment is cheap, and the train to New
York is just two blocks from our house. The job was the best I ever
had, more fun and more challenging than I could have hoped for,
and a much-maligned city is eager for your love. It's easy to feel
useful. Besides, I can shop at Whole Foods on the way home from a
suburban doctor's office, or have a ten dollar cocktail at an upscale
bar nearby. I get to live here as long as I want, but I'll never have to
be from here.

I hadn't been surprised when Chanel's[1] parents wanted a parent-teacher conference after the second marking period report cards came out. Her grade had dropped from a B to a D between November and January, and the offending project—the black hole of a zero that dragged her whole average down—hadn't come early enough for a timely phone call to rectify. I gave her an open-ended extension, and was caught off-guard when she didn't hand anything in by the last day of the cycle. I should have called home. I usually err on the side of trusting my students too much, even though at seventeen they're developmentally still kids, too childish to know that good intentions aren't the same as good habits.

We had our meeting in the office of the school social worker, a very kind woman who had a good relationship with Chanel. Chanel didn't live with her father (and still doesn't—she's now a student at a private college in Virginia), and I knew from some of her past comments that they had very little contact, so it struck me as odd that Mr. Westman came to meet with me. I was nonplussed when he opened with the question, "What exactly is it that you teach my daughter?"

"AP Literature and Composition," I answered. "It's a college level English class."

His brow furrowed. "May I have a moment to confer with my daughter?" he asked, the words big square blocks in his mouth.

The social worker and I sat in awkward silence. I always feel vaguely *in trouble* at parent conferences. Just as I was becoming maddeningly self-conscious about a tiny pull in the elbow of my sweater, Mr. Westman ducked back in, folding his tall, lanky frame into a chair.

"Tell me about the GDA," he said.

I don't know what it's like to have an out teacher. I went to Catholic school. All of the sisters looked like lesbians: they wore sturdy jersey and denim separates and styled their hair in gray bowl cuts, if you could call it "styling." As far as we knew, none of them were gay. To us they were sexless. As for us, we tested out calling ourselves bisexual, half out of boredom and half out of a real fear of the seriousness, the finality, of sex with boys. But when a fast-burning rumor about a lesbian encounter at a sleepover party resulted in a stern warning that girls "like that" didn't belong in our school, I wasn't involved, and was shamefacedly relieved.

My college friends—many of whom survived their big public high schools on the whisper of innuendo that a favorite teacher might be gay—hold that there are two kinds of lesbian teachers: those who dream of saving Radcliffe Hall from her *Well,* and those who would give anything to play doubles with Billie Jean. I'm not the sporty type; until quite recently, I thought a double bagel was just a really, really big breakfast, and I can think of far better ways to spend two hours with the estimable Ms. King.

I didn't want to play the role of the wistful depressed spinster, either, though. The grade school playground was full of taunts at my bookishness. It takes a whole lot of fishnets and whiskey to recover from that sort of thing, and I wasn't about to do any backsliding. Instead, I modeled my classroom persona on what I like to think of as the "household name" approach, popularized by the Ellen Degenereses and Neil Patrick Harrises of the world. The philosophy is simple: Just act natural. You belong here. Live out loud.

I threaded my breath in between dry lips. Mr. Westman may have gotten the name wrong, but I knew immediately what he meant. I pretended I didn't, though, to buy myself a moment.

"The GDA," he insisted. "What's that?"

"Do you mean the GSA? The Gay-Straight Alliance?"

"That's it." He settled back in his seat with a highly satisfied expression on his face. "And that's where you teach them homosexual behavior? Homosexual activities?"

"That's not what it's for," I said, trying to keep the sharpness out of my voice. "It's a program that provides support for LGBT youth and their allies."

The social worker flicked panicked eyes from me to Mr. Westman, her voice tentative and incredulous at once. "It's a national program. And it's not just here—it's all over the district."

"Well," Mr. Westman said, "I might just have to go to the board about that."

In truth, GSA's were not all over our district. In the '09-'10 school year, there was only one—ours—and during the previous school year, we'd been one of only two out of the district's more than ten high schools. The other was shut down after a parent complained that a child who was coincidentally a member of the club had been interviewed in Greenwich Village. The topic of that article was the dearth of activities for LGBT youth in our city. Shutting down a GSA like that is illegal, but I got it when the untenured advisor of that club settled for keeping an eye on his kids informally. You have to keep a little for yourself.

According to GLSEN, the Gay Lesbian Straight Education Network, slightly more than one third of students in the United States attend a school with a Gay-Straight Alliance[2]. GLSEN's 2007 *National Climate Survey* seeks primarily to establish, as the title suggests, the national climate, but it does confirm what you might guess about gender- and sexuality-based harassment specifically in urban schools: the more community members living below the poverty line, the more hostile the environment can be. Harassment for gender expression, sexuality, and racial and ethnic identity are all significantly more common. Discouragingly, LGBT youth experience high levels of truancy, and are twice as likely as their peers to report no post-secondary school aspirations.

Chanel, it should be said, is not queer, or even questioning. As Bonnie Magnuson, a dear, dear friend and director emeritus of GLSEN Northern NJ once said, "The vast majority of GSA members are straight girls. They see it as a social justice issue." That's exactly how Chanel sees it.

Her father, on the other hand, saw it more as an issue of deviance, one he had a lot to say about, and I listened to all of it.

True stories never work out right. Their narratives don't make sense. In this story, there's a big hole in characterization, a glaring incongruity in the fabric of the tale. I come out during job interviews. I switch from ordinary citizen to a mobile safer-sex educator with a moment's notice. I once badgered a class of middle schoolers into jeering, "That's so *homophobic!*" because they were tired of being told not to say, "That's so gay!" This time, though, I sat for almost two hours while an arrogant, bigoted man talked in circles, attacking me and my work. If this were Hollywood, the producers would be firing me and bringing in a replacement who could come up with a script that made sense.

The truth is that I never needed to buy time. The first time Mr. Westman said GDA, I knew what he meant, and I didn't need to collect my thoughts. I made him repeat himself because I wanted him to feel stupid. I did it again and again. I said things like "affective learning" and "pedagogical outcomes" and "deconstructing heteronormative cultural precepts."

I am an educated white woman, and not only am I enjoying a middle class standard of living but I was privileged to have been raised middle class, with the cultural literacies that come with it. My gender presentation is feminine; I can pass as straight any time I want to. My all-access pass to America could probably only be upgraded if I started wearing a clergy collar. Mr. Westman is a black man with a faint accent, maybe Aruban or Jamaican: black *and* foreign. He's imposingly tall, a man with the kind of bulk that makes girls who look like me cross the street in some towns. His caramel-colored jacket looked dusty at the seams, and his fingernails were dirty. I don't remember what I was wearing, which is a luxury, a privilege, in itself. I can attend important meetings without worrying about whether my clothes will be appropriate. I have enough nice clothes that I had plenty to choose from.

In person, I can be earnest and gracious. It comes naturally to me to be generous with compliments and light touches to the shoulder or arm. I laugh easily. Charming parents easily is a point of pride with me, because—well, because who wants to be seen as an arrogant intellectual elitist? More than that, though, I love the families I work with. It's not an act, and it's not charity. I'm lucky to get to hang out with their kids. I admire them, feel pride for them, and most of the time they can make me laugh in the big, gasping guffaws that remind me that all of this is supposed to be fun, and we're in it together. But the breath Mr. Westman expelled saying "GDA" was enough to blow that all away. Suddenly, I wanted to crush him, to send him crawling back to his home, his job, with the certainty that no matter what he believed, my place and my world view were secure. That he was nothing.

Not much actual crushing went on. It was more like this:

Him: "I don't know what your, what your personal habits are, or how you were raised, but one of the things I was raised on was to do right, and to say what's right, no matter how unpopular it is, and I know I speak for all of the parents when I say that we wouldn't want to know that an abomination was being held up as a, as a role model, when the true purpose of education is to show young people what is right. And only the very, very honorable, only the trustworthy, can be responsible for teaching our children right and wrong. Because that is at the center of everything they will do for the rest of their lives. So when a child gets the idea in school that a kind of lifestyle that is the opposite of society's beliefs is actually an okay way to live, then that means that there's a, a rotten hole in the center of their learning. And we can't allow that to continue. Do you know what I'm saying?"

Me: "It sounds like you're saying that because I believe in gay rights

I can't help the kids become good people."

Him: "You're twisting my words."

Social Worker: "."

Nice assist, lady. Thanks a lot. Now lather, rinse, repeat. Forty times.

Beneath the rhetoric and the talking points, between the verbal acrobatics and the euphemisms and the awkward, pregnant pauses, the crux of it came out. At some point, Chanel permitted her father to believe that I was using *The Picture of Dorian Gray* to teach homosexual themes. She did this despite knowing that he was rabidly homophobic (as, incidentally, the book is). She probably never expected that he'd actually come from New York to confront me.

Casting doubt on the teacher is the first line of defense for a kid who smells a bad grade coming. Maybe she was truly afraid of his fury, and I saved her from a beating, or maybe she was just idly talking, goading him. Maybe it was thrilling to argue with him about gay rights at the dinner table, until things got out of control and he took it seriously. Maybe he's very religious, and she's just beginning to resist church-going. Maybe he's a closet case, and she finally told him about me and the book and the GSA because he wouldn't stop bugging her about whether any of her friends were gay. Maybe she needed the shouting to stop, for once.

I always had a soft spot for Chanel because she had an exuberant way of reading, as if each book and its coiled world were a treasure left particularly for her. She was charming and needy. She never felt that she could keep up with the other students in our class. Once she told me, "I don't ever want to say anything, because I can't talk like them, but then I get so into it I feel like I *have* to say something—and then they laugh at me!" I could never catch the other kids laughing at her, but I don't discredit her. It happens a lot. She was a little rough, and her work habits were poor, but her insights were incisive and radical.

Between her father, our class, and me, she was in a tough position, so even when I was still dazed from the meeting, I wasn't mad at her. I could have felt spiteful, or resentful, but I didn't. The only feeling I had was fear. I never kicked that. What kind of teacher feels so much anxiety in the face of a student that she can't muster empathy?

At long last, Mr. Westman conceded that I might not be all bad. This was long after he gave up on getting me to promise to stop teaching *Dorian Gray*, and I had given up on bashing him over the head with my ten-dollar words. It was only making things worse. We were both parched. We'd spent the better part of an afternoon together. Perhaps, he offered, perhaps I wanted to do the right thing, but like water seeping through a crack in the sidewalk, my proclivities would sneak through, whether I wanted them to or not. I couldn't help teaching the kids to be gay. I think he believed that if he admitted that I wasn't being intentionally harmful that I might meet him in the middle and quit my job. Eventually we just tired each other out, and left. The social worker was really relieved.

Afterward, I did the right things. I told my union rep what had happened, and filed an affirmative action report. I told my direct supervisor. A few days later, one of the building's vice principals took me aside and told me gruffly that he was sorry to hear what I was going through. I didn't ask what he meant, although I immediately wished that I had. I hated myself for succumbing to the worldwide, open-ended gag order on homophobia. In fact, I wished that I hadn't let the whole episode push me and pull me into so many funny shapes: mean, disdainful, frightened, and embarrassed. It cracked me, and my proclivities seeped through, just like he said.

Because I am a queer teacher, I cannot teach books like *The Picture of Dorian Gray* without justifying their inclusion in the curriculum. I cannot be certain that my efforts to teach civic engagement and ethics as part of an affective skill set will be viewed as genuine and unbiased. Like queer members of all professions, I cannot rely on accepted institutional practices and policies to combat discrimination to protect me. But I also cannot expect my experiences as a queer teacher to provide me with adequate tools to see and master the vast privilege that I bring to my work. I cannot permit myself to use my privilege to further leverage oppression, even in the guise of undermining homophobia. Instead, let me learn to make my teaching a practice of humility, kindness, courage, and solidarity.

Notes

1. Names have been changed and a non-participating character omitted.
2. Kosciw, J. G., Diaz, E. M., and Greytak, E. A. (2008). *2007 National School Climate Survey: The experiences of lesbian, gay, bisexual and transgender youth in our nation's schools*. New York: GLSEN.

A Teacher's Lesson
Lissa Brown

❦

Intended as a warning to secondary teaching majors to avoid career-crippling litigation, a college professor in an instructional methods course said, "Never touch a student." I read with horror the required articles in National Education Association journals and other publications about teachers who had faced false allegations of improper physical contact with students and lost their jobs.

As a college senior flushed with the success of my recent student teaching experience and eager to begin my teaching career, I found it disturbing to think all my hard work could be for naught if a vindictive student pinned a target on my back. "All it takes is an accusation," my professor warned. When it comes to this issue, he assured us, facts were completely irrelevant.

I adhered steadfastly to the "don't touch" rule through most of my years as a high school history teacher. I prayed my comforting touch to a girl having an epileptic seizure in my classroom would be overlooked, and that my amateur, hands-on ministrations to a child who'd caught her hand in a bicycle chain in the parking lot would not mark the end of my teaching career.

Ever mindful of the consequences of being branded a child molester by suspicious students or parents, I followed the advice I received as a college senior. But no one ever prepared me for the insidious behavior of parents who might be suspicious of my friendship with another female teacher or warned me that it could affect my teaching.

To set the record straight, I taught in two public school systems in New Jersey over a period of seventeen plus years. During that time I did not identify as a lesbian. I dated men and for most of that time denied the possibility that I might be sexually attracted to women. I participated in many consciousness-raising activities through NOW and other organizations and somehow managed to steer clear of confronting my own orientation issues. Fear of seeing my teaching career come to a screeching halt probably contributed to that situation.

In September of 1969, a mere three months after the Stonewall riots in nearby New York City had raised everyone's awareness of gays and lesbians, I began a new teaching job. A woman in my department had agreed to mentor me, since I was new to the school system. Carol and I had a lot in common. We taught the same subjects, had similar ethnic backgrounds, and loved to travel. We soon began spending time together on weekends and planned trips to Europe, Asia and the Middle East during our spring and summer breaks. We both had strong advocacy interests and advanced to fill leadership positions in the teacher's union.

Hoping to maintain my interest in teaching, I developed a new course, *The American Woman*. If not the first, it was among the initial women's studies courses in American public high schools. I was told it would live or die based on student enrollment and was confident I could interest enough students to elect the course.

At about the same time this new course was offered, the union's battles with the school board and superintendent rose to a fever pitch. Much was written in the local newspapers about union leaders, including me, and systematic rumors were floated about our private lives. One persistent rumor linked Carol and me in a lesbian relationship. While there was absolutely no truth to the rumor, it continued and spread through and beyond the school district.

Discussions in my classroom were notable for the complete absence of any topic that might touch on lesbianism. Naturally, students in this course were curious about some of the women we studied. In particular, some questioned why so many of the women were unmarried. When students asked questions about hints of lesbianism in literature they were reading, I dodged them. I was uncomfortable doing that, something I'd never had to do before in my classroom. My own fears about being charged with proselytizing a lesbian lifestyle led me to rob my students of a potentially rich discussion.

There was no basic textbook in that course. I'd deliberately avoided using one because I wanted students to become familiar with the ballooning body of literature about women who had changed our history. I divided the course into two sections; the first was a review of notable women in our history and their accomplishments.

The second part of the course covered a variety of topics that emphasized a sociological approach. We examined the evolving roles of women as portrayed in mass media, advertising and the workforce, and tackled some controversial issues such as abortion and discrimination based on gender.

I recall an instance when a student questioned something she read about a prominent woman who became president of one of the early women's colleges. The article she read used the expression a "Boston marriage" to describe her domestic arrangement with another woman. She wanted to know what that meant. I answered very carefully, avoiding the term "lesbian." I knew I conveyed the point when another student chimed in saying something like, "Oh, you mean they were lesbians?" I remember walking over to my classroom door and shutting it, fearing the consequences if my department head happened to walk by and hear that word. "Some people thought so," I answered, and did not elaborate.

Teachers love those "teachable moments" that occur from time to time. That was a great one, and I could have used it to explore a variety of issues involving societal attitudes and how they were changing, but I didn't dare.

There were a few lesbians in my class and I felt I cheated them of their right to know many of the influential women in our history who braved discrimination in order to follow their path. How sad that I wasn't willing to risk losing my livelihood to provide that.

One day as I was preparing to leave school, one of our guidance counselors stopped me and asked if we could talk. We walked to her office and I sat down. This was not a colleague with whom I had a particularly close relationship, so I was a bit surprised when she pulled her chair out from behind her desk and sat next to me. I soon realized why she'd done that. She was about to deliver bad news.

She explained that she received calls from the parents of two students in my American Woman class, insisting they wanted to take their daughters out of the class. "Why?" I asked. She beat around the bush, trying to avoid telling me what they had really said, but I got the message. Apologetically, she told me the parents alluded to their belief that I lived with Carol and they didn't want me influencing their daughters. I told her Carol and I had never lived together and urged her to look up our records. We didn't even live in the same town.

"What did you tell them?" I demanded. I wanted to hear her explanation, suspecting I already knew the answer. She explained that she tried to dissuade them but they were adamant. Since it was an elective course and neither student needed the credits to graduate, she caved to their demands. She declined my offer to speak with the parents and to urge them to consider the students' opinions. I knew the girls did not want to leave the class. In fact, the next day one of them came to me after school to apologize and told me how sorry she was to have to drop the class. I told her I was sorry too and that I understood that she had to bow to parental pressure.

I'm not sure how much influence these events had on my eventual decision to leave the teaching profession. I always believed I had given my students my best and encouraged them to have open minds. I had a reputation for being forthright. I felt somewhat ashamed to face the fact that when it came to the subject of lesbianism, I took the safe route to preserve my job.

It's difficult to know how much the denial of my own lesbianism contributed to my behavior in the classroom. Within one year of the experiences described above, I began the journey leading to my own coming out. I struggled as most people do who wait until they are nearly forty years old to face their feelings. By that time I was safely employed in the private sector in a new career. Far from the schoolhouse door, I shed the baggage of self-denial and recognized myself for who I am, a lesbian.

One opportunity to atone for the dishonesty in the classroom came unexpectedly when I ran into a former student. Terri was a bright student whom I taught in three different grades. We kept in touch after she graduated and she came to the school to visit me from time to time. As I was packing my personal files on my last day of teaching, she helped carry boxes down three flights of steps to my car. We said our goodbyes in the parking lot, promising to remain in touch, and I left behind my role of teacher.

I suspected two things about Terri when she was my student; she was a lesbian, and she had a crush on me. Several months later we got together for dinner and I invited her to join me at a swim club on the weekend. I enjoyed hearing about her success at NYU and then the conversation turned more personal.

"I've always trusted you to tell the truth," she said. "You're one of few teachers I've had whose honesty I'd bet on."

"Well thanks," I replied cautiously, suspecting I'd be tested at any moment.

"So, can I ask you a question?"

"Sure, go ahead," I replied.

Nervously she continued. "So, was there any truth to the rumors about you and Carol?"

I took a deep breath and looked her in the eye. "No, not a word of truth," I answered, "but I've been doing a lot of self-examination and am exploring the possibility that I do prefer women."

She looked relieved.

Now it was my turn. "Why do you ask? Is it merely idle curiosity?"

Her red face provided all the answer I needed but she replied, "No, I guess I wanted to know if we were birds of a feather…"

"I'd say that's a very real possibility," I answered.

It seemed a natural follow-up to our conversation; I asked her to accompany me to a women's bookstore. Old habits die hard and I was intent on doing some reading before plunging into the lesbian world. I asked if she could recommend a couple of good books. Together we browsed the collection and she suggested I purchase a copy of *The Coming Out Stories*. We laughed at the apparent role reversal inherent in that field trip.

Shortly afterwards, I introduced Terri to my new lover, the woman who has been my partner for twenty-seven years. We went to an off-off-Broadway production of the play *Sisters* together and I enjoyed the mutual embarrassment as we three neophyte lesbians watched a nude love scene between two nuns.

Through subsequent conversations I realized Terri had regarded me as a role model. I've wondered how much easier I could have made her life if I'd been more conscious of my own orientation and been willing to speak of the unspeakable in my classroom. Thirty years later, however, I'm comfortable with the knowledge that she has forgiven my failing and we remain good friends.

Physical Education
Cynthia Tyler

❦

The first time I saw Penny Finch she was demonstrating her backswing to a line of apathetic teenage girls. I studied her toned, tan legs, ankle socks with navy blue pom poms, clean sneakers, and white sleeveless blouse tucked into light blue culottes. She had medium-length brown hair bleached by the sun, and a chirpy voice with an accent that didn't sound like anybody I knew in California. I was one floor above her that day, my first day of high school. I'd just left the attendance office where the clerk had been examining the note from my mother like it was a counterfeit twenty.

"See you next week," she said, and dismissed the class with a flourish of the tennis racket. I heard the swish as it cut through the air. She must have felt me watching her, because she glanced up for a second, then turned and walked toward the girl's gym.

I double-timed it down the stairs and followed the group into the locker room, and then trudged up to the second floor faculty office. My knock echoed on the metal doorframe and she looked at me from her desk with dawn-blue eyes so clear and deep they gave me a start. She was wearing lip-gloss, like a lot of women did back then, in a shade that made her look like she'd just kissed a dish of peach sorbet.

"Yes ma'am?" The formal greeting threw me off.

"I need you to sign my absence card." I held it out, willing my hand not to shake. The rumble of voices from the locker room below reverberated up the stairs and swallowed my voice. I had to repeat myself.

She took the card and laid it in the center of her desk, then leaned on her elbows with her chin perched on her fist, examining it. "Ah, Tyler. I wondered what became of you. Did your cruise ship get into port late?"

"Sick." I coughed into my fist and looked away.

She shook her head and sighed, like she had to wonder what kind of pitiful specimen of youth couldn't drag its carcass in for the first week of classes. She initialed the card and handed it back to me. "We'll be in the pool starting Monday. Bring your suit next week."

"The pool?" My stomach fell.

"Yes, ma'am, the pool." She stood, arched an eyebrow and gave me a quick once- over. I felt somebody behind me and was jostled forward by a tall senior with a tight, tanned body wearing a purple Speedo, her long blonde hair shedding droplets of chlorine-scented water all over my book bag.

"Hey, McGee." Finch picked up a whistle and a clipboard and spoke to the girl. "We missed you at practice last week. I guess you and Tyler here were having so much fun on that cruise ship you figured school could wait."

McGee giggled and plopped down in Finch's chair, depositing her bare feet on the desk in the spot where my absence card had been. My face felt red and hot as I backed out of the room.

"Out of my chair, brat," Finch said, and their laughter followed me down the stairs.

Finch was in her early thirties, a recent arrival from Michigan, and divorced. She drove a convertible red sports car too fast through the faculty parking lot. I'd heard about her from my older female high school friends over the summer. I also heard that she had a special friendship with one of her students, a girl named Diane, who'd graduated a year before. The former star of the girl's swim team, Diane was described to me as a burly super jock with short hair whose mother was worried enough about the relationship to telephone some of the other mothers and discuss her concerns. Nobody ever said the word "lesbian" but it hung in the air like the brownish-gray layer of smog over the San Fernando Valley.

Gay people were mostly invisible to me that fall of 1975, my sophomore year in high school. The first lesbian love story on national television, *The War Widow*, wouldn't appear until the following year. When it finally aired, I sat mesmerized in front of the portable TV in my bedroom and watched for a solid week. Every time PBS would repeat it, I was there in front of the television, trying to decide which of the two women I found more attractive—Jenny, the photographer or Amy, the lonely widow of the WW1 soldier. (I chose Jenny.) Harvey Milk hadn't yet been elected Supervisor up north in San Francisco, and the Briggs Initiative, which attempted to ban anyone who supported gay rights from working in the California public school system, was three years off. The only Stonewall I'd ever heard of was a Confederate general in the Civil War.

I'd kissed a girl, my best friend Kathy, for the first time the year before, but she hadn't registered for school that year and disappeared from my life. The last I'd heard, her mother had taken her to some kind of counseling that took place on a floor below the police station. I hoped this turn of events had nothing to do with me and all the letters and phone calls exchanged between us, but it weighed on my mind. In truth, my absence during the first several days of school had nothing to do with physical illness. I'd been so distraught over losing Kathy that I was unable to sleep or hold down food. My parents were starting to watch me anxiously, remarking on the dark circles under my eyes and the way my clothes hung on my body. They were relieved to collude with my false report of an early season flu bug.

I knew I was gay like I knew the alphabet. On school nights I would lay on my madras print bed cover, listening to Jackson Browne or The Divine Miss M on the turntable, and flipping through the paperback poetry anthologies that I'd pick up on weekends at Pickwick Books in Hollywood when I'd make the trip with my straight friends who thought I had exotic literary taste: *Psyche: The Feminine Poetic Consciousness*, *We Become New*, *Rising Tides*. I read Judy Grahn's *Common Woman Poems* out loud to myself frequently, the portraits of women so alive I felt like I could touch them. I read those books like dying people read the bible, a shaky index finger running under a line of prose, whispering the words to myself, scribbling in the margins, studying the grainy black and white author photos. I imagined what it would be like to have these women as friends, as lovers. Here was my tribe, a web of women known only on the slim pages of a book, but I felt connection all the same.

As I lay there missing Kathy, my thoughts returned to Penny Finch's pretty face, and despite my guilt, I envisioned romantic scenes with Penny instead of Kathy. Could the rumors be true? Soon my thoughts were intruded by the image of super jock leaning forward to receive a swimming medal, performing a triple back flip off the high dive, or carrying the Olympic torch while Finch beamed and applauded from the sidelines. How could I ever compete?

I'd had no success or interest in sports. Volleyball, paddleball, badminton, track. Who would invent such stupid ways to spend time? I thought of the steam rising off the pool in the morning air, the deep green water choppy after the swimmers pulled their lean and muscular bodies from the racing lanes. I imagined standing in front of Finch in my bathing suit, complete with nose clip and latex swim cap. As a preview of coming attractions, I pulled the ugly suit over my soft, white body and stood in front of the full-length bathroom mirror for the total effect. I pinched my nose shut with my fingers and said "Good morning, Miss Finch" in a nasal voice to the mirror. Swimming itself wasn't the problem. I flailed around in the water without any grace at all, but I knew enough to keep from drowning. It was the idea of looking like a dork in front of Penny Finch that I couldn't bear.

I decided not to swim. I had P.E. for first period, so I began to skip it. Instead, I'd go to a neighborhood bakery that had a few tables and read my copy of Sylvia Plath's *Ariel* over black coffee, trying to look like a community college student. Or I'd sit on a curb in the empty grocery store parking lot and pull a *Creem* Magazine out of my Pee Chee folder, light up a Marlboro, and read about Patti Smith, Lou Reed, Alice Cooper, and The Rolling Stones. Stamping out my cigarette, I'd plug a piece of Trident into my mouth and rush back to class barely in time for second period Spanish.

It took *weeks* before I was caught!

And then one day, right before lunch, as I sat half-snoozing over *The Red Badge of Courage* in fourth period American Lit, a skinny girl with a Farrah Fawcett haircut walked into the room and handed a note to the teacher. He unfolded it and looked at me.

"Tyler. Vice Principal Wolfe's office. Move it."

I gulped a lungful of stale classroom air that always smelled faintly of tuna fish and Twinkies, closed the book, grabbed my purse, and walked the maze of hallways to the administrator's offices, anxiety roaring in my ears like the world's scariest conch shell.

Wolfe led me directly into her office. She was a thin, leathery woman with sharp features and gray hair pulled back in a tight bun.

"Miss Finch assumed you'd transferred to another school and that the attendance sheets she continued to receive with your name on them reflected a clerical error. She decided to double check with the office this morning." Wolfe steepled her fingertips and, rocked back in her leather executive chair, managing to frown while looking slightly amused at the same time. I stayed silent.

"Why didn't you go to class?" She had a smoker's voice, and I wondered what would happen if I leaned forward and shook one out of my pack for her.

"I don't know how to swim," I said.

She tapped a pen on her desk and considered my answer. I watched the red second hand of the clock travel from 3 to 6.

"But learning is the whole point of school."

I shrugged, and stood there. She hadn't invited me to sit. She seemed anxious to be somewhere else, like back to the faculty lounge for another puff. What could I say? *I'm crushing on Finch and I don't want her to see me in a bathing suit* seemed like it might create an even bigger problem for me.

"Unfortunately, however, you've missed the opportunity. The class has moved on to badminton. You missed tennis, too, by the way. I'm expecting you to report to Ms. Finch tomorrow morning. She'll have your make-up assignment ready for you."

"What will I have to do?" I blurted out the question in a panic, as it occurred to me how many laps around the track I'd have to run to make up two months of P.E. They'd probably make me swim to Hawaii and back, or assign me twelve million push-ups, or five thousand jumping jacks.

Wolfe tapped her pen against the lip of her coffee cup like she was ashing a Virginia Slims. She looked at me with a kink in her eyebrow. "I'm afraid you'll have to write essays. Many of them."

Finch was subdued the next morning when I stood in the doorway to her office dressed in my gym clothes, waiting for my make-up assignment. She didn't call me "ma'am" or "Tyler" or anything else, but instead handed me a piece of lined notebook paper on which she'd handwritten my essay topics. How did Earth Day change the nation? How did Richard Nixon's resignation affect the notion of presidential powers? What is Plato's *Allegory of the Cave* and how is it important in today's world? What is the difference between propaganda, advocacy, and yellow journalism? How might the recent OPEC oil embargo transform political and economic power relations between the industrialized nations and the Third World?

I read over the questions for a few minutes, blinked hard, and tucked the paper in my folder.

"And that's just for starters." The voice startled me and I turned and saw a girl in shorts and a muscle t-shirt sitting at one of the teacher's desks, arms folded behind her head, laughing.

"That's enough, Diane," Finch muttered.

"Right." I gave her a friendly nod and went back to my locker.

After that I started showing up for gym class every day, and I even had a pretty good time pounding the birdie with the thin wooden racket. I was assigned a partner and we played a doubles tournament, coming in second place among the class of thirty. Sometimes when we'd finish our games early we'd take laps around the track and if Finch was watching I'd make an effort, or someone would put Elton John's "Crocodile Rock" on the record player and we'd do aerobic exercises to the music. I wasn't much of an athlete, but I could dance pretty well. I began to get a bit of color in my face and felt more energetic. But I never once got a reaction out of Finch for any of these new feats of physical prowess.

Diane would appear in front of the class occasionally. Although she'd graduated the previous year, she still hung around Finch, who would sometimes disappear and leave her in charge of the class, handing over the whistle and the clipboard in a symbolic transition of power. They didn't look like lovers, they didn't act like lovers, but according to gossip they were inseparable on the weekends. This, I knew, proved nothing, even if it was true. Still, I ached with jealousy.

In order to complete my lengthy make-up assignment by the deadline, I bought a thick notebook and wrote in the bathtub, at the dinner table, in the backseat of my Mom's Chrysler New Yorker on the way to the orthodontist. I began to enjoy articulating my opinions on the various topics of the day, trying different styles of writing, all while single-mindedly focused on my audience of one. One Saturday night I found a marijuana roach my older brother had stashed in the loving cup of his tennis trophy and I smoked it standing in my bedroom closet to hide the smell of weed from my parents. I wanted to see if my writing would improve by dimming the lights and playing Pink Floyd's "Dark Side of the Moon" album on low in the background, but I found out soon enough that the muse didn't appear when I was zonked on pot. I went to bed early and started over again the next day, clear-eyed and sober.

When I was finally finished I turned in eight multiple-page essays in eight neat Smead fastener folders on topics ranging from politics to the environment to astronomy and modern jazz. On the day they were due I stacked them neatly in the center of Finch's desk and promptly forgot about them.

A week later, I was standing by the drinking fountain when Finch walked up to me. As usual, my heart began to pound and my legs turned to spaghetti. She wasn't smiling.

"Your essays are very good. Are you sure you wrote them yourself?"

I started to protest, and then realized with regret that skipping class had thrown my entire reputation into question.

I looked her in the eye. "Yes."

"Are you going to be a writer?" The question startled and embarrassed me. I'd never considered the possibility.

"I don't know. Maybe."

She gave me an odd look. "Well, think about it."

I felt myself pump up a bit and started to say something else when she blew her whistle six inches from my ear. "All right people! Listen up! I want three laps around the track and then get your butts out of my sight until tomorrow."

Finch and I began to exchange reading material. She brought me her English textbooks from college, and I'd sit in bed at night reading them, thrilled that they'd once been in her hands. I pretended that Henry James wasn't boring and tedious and thanked her for bringing them all the way to school for me. I loaned her the novels I was reading, crinkly paperback copies of *On The Road, Slaughterhouse Five*, and a copy of Kate Chopin's *The Awakening* that she told me she loved, except for the ending. Other than that one time, she never commented on any of the books I loaned her, and I wondered if she read them.

Whatever her relationship with Diane, her behavior toward me was never anything but professional. I continued to fantasize about the two of us zipping up the coast to Big Sur in her sports car, spinning around curves, the wind in our hair, like something out of a Prince Matchabelli ad for White Musk cologne. Until one day a quiet girl named Megan walked into the gym wearing a peasant skirt and a pair of high-heeled Frye boots, and introduced herself as a transfer from the Bay area. Megan was also in my creative writing class and the two of us began working on the class literary magazine together after school. Soon after Megan arrived she and Penny were sharing space in my daydreams.

The year-end class party was held at the swimming pool. I attended, wearing cut-off 501s and a halter top instead of the dowdy bathing suit, which I'd rolled up and stashed on the top shelf of my closet in a box with my old Halloween costumes from grade school.

Squiggles of white light danced around on the concrete near the pool where students had laid out beach towels and somebody's transistor radio was playing the Eagles "Best of My Love" that day in mid-June when I took a deep breath and approached Penny Finch for the last time that year.

"I'm really sorry about not coming to class for all those weeks. I wanted to thank you for letting me make up the time."

She'd been staring out at the Verdugo Mountains with a faraway look in her eyes and it appeared I'd interrupted deep thoughts. "Are you going to tell me why you went AWOL?" she asked, turning to face me.

"Nope."

I hugged her, a long, tight embrace that made a couple of heads turn, and she hugged me back. Then I jumped in the water, and swam over to where Megan was sitting at the edge of the pool, legs dangling over the side, watching me out of the corner of her eye.

Teaching Out
B.J. Epstein

‹›

One thing I can't stand in a teacher is soapboxing. That is to say, when a teacher gives the class her or his own opinions on political or social issues, or even talks about her or his own personal experiences, using valuable class time as a chance to convince students to think one way or another about certain subjects. Or at least I used to think that. While I'd still say that it is wrong to impose ideas on students, I've started to realize that we teachers have a duty to open their eyes about and to the world, to offer them new perspectives and new understandings, to give them the opportunity to realize that their way of life isn't the only way, or necessarily the right way. And sometimes this might mean making topics more personal than we—or the students, or our colleagues— might find comfortable.

My university students often seem surprisingly unaware of gender and sexuality issues. My female students blithely refer to themselves as "girls" (a term I dislike because it diminishes the adulthood of women) and announce that they are "real girly girls" because they wear pink and took ballet lessons as a child. Meanwhile, I'm told that "real guys" play football and enjoy watching sports, and even though female students far outnumber male ones in literature courses, no one comments on the fact that the males dominate the classroom, interrupting the females, talking loudly, and speaking for much more of the time than the women do. I see how the young women preen for the young men, playing with their hair, crossing and re-crossing their legs, trying to get their attention, instead of focusing on our class discussion. So there is a clear gender divide in classes that seems very old-fashioned and depressing to me, although when I try to connect this to what we are reading—to take George Eliot's novel *Daniel Deronda* as an example, I asked the students to consider whether they feel that women today have fewer expectations upon them and more opportunities than unhappy Gwendolen did—I was told that "no one thinks like that anymore" and that "women can do everything and be anything today." Maybe the students truly feel this way, or maybe they are just repeating what they've been told, but they sure don't act like it. Nor are they conscious of the fact that this may not be the case for all women, in all classes, in all societies. On top of that, the students tell me they cannot understand why anyone "would want to read a book by a feminist or a lesbian" or a book about such people. My female students admit to me, without an ounce of embarrassment, that they don't talk as much when there are males around, because they wouldn't want the men to believe that they're "radical feminists" or "man-haters," simply because they dare to show their intelligence or their independent thinking.

Here, then, I am left in a quandary. I wonder whether I should come out to my students as both a feminist and a queer woman and, if so, exactly what to say. And if I don't, how can I make the political and the social personal? How can I make them open their eyes when they don't realize that their eyes are even closed?

For one particular class, I initially kept my comments general, probably too general. Talking about sex—which you are implicitly doing as soon as you begin discussing gender roles, stereotypes, and behaviors—may not be appropriate in class, although to say that in itself raises additional issues and questions in my mind about what is appropriate and why and who decided that. And as this group of students was especially caught in the old pattern of being taken aback when asked to examine their views, instead of telling the students anything about my experience as a woman, and a queer one at that, I asked them more questions, to try to get them to think more widely and deeply about the issues. But that didn't seem to do enough, even if it did start some worthwhile discussions. So I changed my tactic.

As is the teacher's prerogative, I gave my students some additional reading that I thought would be beneficial and I carefully led class discussion so that issues of sexuality and gender—as related to the theoretical and literary texts we were reading—came up, and, so to speak, came out. With Eliot's *Deronda*, the students kept saying that the moralistic message bothered them and that it had nothing to do with their times. They insisted again that there was little discrimination today and that people won't drop a friend if they found out the friend was "Jewish or whatever," as happened in the novel. So I told them that on the contrary, I'd had friends cut off contact with me, although not because I was culturally Jewish; rather, people had broken off friendships when I had come out as queer. There was a shocked silence as the students digested this information, in terms of both my gayness and what had happened. Then one admitted that she had a gay older sister and that her sister had faced discrimination. Another said she thought her parents wouldn't mind if she came home with a black man, but they would object if she came home with a woman. We were able to compare all this to the situation in *Deronda*, where Christian parents didn't want their children to marry Jews, and to the situation in Jim Crow America, when blacks and whites could not legally marry. There was a distressed murmur as my students began to realize that the world was not as overflowing with equality as they had thought it was; earlier in the session, they'd been saying how irrelevant books such as Eliot's were to life today, and now they were angrily pointing out that things hadn't moved on as much as they had thought. And this disappointed and deflated them, but I would argue that such a reality check was useful. And it wouldn't have come about if I had kept quiet.

For two of my introductory literature classes, I chose to assign my students theoretical work by Judith Butler and other gender and queer theorists, which I hoped would provide fodder for discussion and for thought. But when I asked about the reading, they said things such as, "Girls are girls, and boys are boys. What's the issue?" One argumentative student wasn't interested in matters of sexuality and he didn't see why we had to discuss it. He claimed he'd never met a lesbian before, but he said he'd seen some, and they "always looked like men." "Really?" I asked him. "What about me? Do I look like one?" The class was flustered and there was an awkward silence, and then suddenly the students began to speak. They wondered why I didn't look like a man, and if I felt like one, and they asked if I'd ever been with a man, and if it was hard being gay, and how I thought about gender, and while I kept my responses short, always referring back to Butler's work as a theoretical basis, my students got more and more engaged. Before long, I was able to shut up and they took over the discussion, debating topics such as the use of our binary gender system and how we socialize children into specific genders and sexualities and if we could rethink gender roles in literature and in society. It was as though me bringing myself briefly into the conversation allowed them to personalize issues that had otherwise seemed distant. Even some of the quieter, self-proclaimed "girly girls" threw themselves into the topics, not seeming to care anymore if the guys thought they were "feminists" just because they talked.

For a class with MA students in literary translation, my approach was different. The students were older and less sheltered, but as with many people, they made heterosexist assumptions. I chose to refer to my then-partner—and I of course used the female pronoun—so I came out in a subtle way, which I hoped would at least make them understand that not everyone lives a heterosexual life. I was pleased when later a student made reference to relationships and carefully named various possible terms and pronouns and how different languages use them. I was glad that I had mentioned something personal, though I had done so as unobtrusively as possible, and that it seemed to have some effect on the students' ways of speaking and thinking. And this experience made me more determined to be open to my students about who I am, if it will make a difference to our discussion and to their understanding.

Outside of class, I try to be as out as possible, too. My colleagues know I research queer studies, among other things, and am involved in lgbt activities, and if they nevertheless assume that I am straight, I gently correct them, such as the time when I was asked if I had a partner and, if so, what "he" did. Also, I have Stonewall's bright red "Some people are gay. Get over it." poster in my office and a similar postcard on my door. Oddly, the postcard keeps getting stolen, and I keep replacing it. I have a rainbow flag on my wall as well. Though I like these things, I keep them primarily for my students and not for me; I want students to feel that they have a teacher they can talk to about these sorts of issues, should they need to, and I also want young queer people to see an example of someone living a healthy, happy, out life. I certainly don't point out the sign or the flag to students during my office hours, but the items are there as a relatively understated hint.

I've begun to think of this as teaching out, by which I mean being out about who and what I am as I teach, and since it has been clearly beneficial both for me and my students, I suspect it might be so for others as well. I don't need to come out to my students in a formal way and I don't want to lecture them on topics such as gay rights or feminism, unless that would be directly relevant to the subject at hand; all I have to do is to accept who I am and to be myself as I teach, and that has made a big difference in my classes.

"Imagine My Surprise"[1]: *Being Out as a Lesbian Teacher, 1990-2010*

Barbara DiBernard

ℰℐ

If there are lesbians on TV, do we still need lesbians in real life? Isn't acceptance and assimilation the big goal?

—*Susanna J. Sturgis*

Sturgis' ironic questions express for me the surprising journey of being an out lesbian teacher for the last twenty years at the University of Nebraska-Lincoln. When I first began coming out in class in the late 1980s, I was the first lesbian or gay person that many students were aware of knowing. For them, I saw myself as Margaret Atwood's "I-Witness," "the one to whom personal experience happens and the one who makes experience personal for others" (348). For the lesbian and gay students, I hope I served as a visible example of an out, proud, politically active, and arguably "successful" lesbian adult. But in 2010, with lesbians on TV, with students downloading "I Kissed a Girl" onto their iPods, and with American Idol finalists coming out as gay, students don't need the same kind of "I-Witness." In fact, many students, including those with same sex partners, reject the labels of "lesbian" and "gay" altogether, along with other identity labels. Students come to class with postmodern notions of identity as multiple, fragmented, and unstable, which they translate to a distrust of all labels as limiting and reductive. I worry that this fragmented postmodern notion of identity has been successfully co-opted by the mainstream and transmuted into a fear of labels that leaves people ostensibly connected to everyone but in reality allied to no one. What I would like to argue here is that we DO need lesbians in real life, and that acceptance and assimilation should NOT be our goals, for they always depend on erasing difference and a lack of analysis of privilege. For more than thirty years lesbians of color have been saying that naming and claiming all of our identities is the means to effective political action. It's more than time that we listened. Being out as lesbian teachers while teaching the herstory of lesbian feminism can be part of this process. I would like to use some stories from and reflections on my 20+ years and ongoing journey as an out lesbian teacher to explore these ideas.

From Audre Lorde, I learned that "the transformation of silence into language and action" is a political act, and a necessary one. I first came out in class and continue to do so in direct response to Lorde's challenge:

> What are the words you do not yet have? What do you need to say? What are the tyrannies you swallow day by day and attempt to make your own, until you will sicken and die of them, still in silence? ("Transformation" 41)

For me, coming out as a lesbian led to a strong sense of being whole for the first time and an integration of what had previously felt like "life" and "work." My teaching, community activism, and participation in a lesbian feminist community became my "work" in Audre Lorde's meaning of the term.[2] As I expressed in my 1990 essay, "Being an I-Witness: My Life as a Lesbian Teacher," I considered being out as a lesbian teacher a central part of that work.

In the early years of being out and into the mid 1990s, many students responded to my being out in the classroom with silence, although it was not unusual for students in Intro to Women's Lit to write in their reading journals or say in class that homosexuals were "sick," "perverted," or "immoral." Other students, trying to be more open-minded, said or wrote that they "just didn't understand homosexuality." Some, though, were outwardly hostile. In 1990, one student wrote in an anonymous end-of-semester evaluation of Introduction to Women's Literature, a sophomore level class:

> I do not think it is appropriate for anyone to read about lesbians and their habits. . . . I realize this is the 90s but there are some of us who still value

decency, purity, chastity, and Christianity. . . . As far as [the teacher's] choice of materials and her own personal convictions, I am violently opposed. Her hero is Audre Lorde—big time lesbian. I find that a problem.

During this time period a male student wrote an article for the school newspaper in which he called a heterosexual colleague of mine a "Femi Nazi," accusing her of forcing a lesbian agenda on the students in Intro to Women Writers by including what he considered an excessive amount of lesbian content in the class.

But the more common dynamic in this course was most students' lack of a daily integrated awareness that some women are lesbians and one could expect to read of their experiences in a women's lit course. In "Being an I-Witness" I give an example of the lengths some students went to in order to place a heterosexual grid over Amy Lowell's poems, in spite of the fact that the intro in our anthology stated that her lover was a woman. Still, by the mid 1990s, students responded to my being out and to reading and discussing lesbian content with decreasing moral outrage. More students came out in class. More students who identified as heterosexual had lesbian sisters, mothers, aunts, or friends who were out to them. It was clear that at least some women writers or characters could be lesbian, or even your classmate or teacher.

I do not want to skim over how hard this time was, though, for me or for lesbian students. While I always had a supportive department chair and colleagues, it took a toll to be battered in this way privately through student journals and evaluations and publicly in class and to respond with attempts at connection, understanding, and education. In addition, students, faculty, and staff endured overt homophobia on campus. In 1997, in response to approved chalkings on National Coming Out Day, others chalked anti-gay sentiments, including "Deer Season = Queer Season." It took the administration what many of us considered an unconscionably long period of time to make any public statement in response. In 2003 someone vandalized an LGBT bulletin board in the English building on campus, tearing down everything on the board, and doing so a second and then a third time after we had restored it. In 2010, we do not yet have domestic partner benefits at our university. Even so-called "soft" benefits, such as funeral leave or family leave, have been denied.

Imagine my surprise, then, when in the 21st century, many students in same sex relationships refused the identities of "lesbian" and "gay," and most students expressed their belief that all identity labels were reductive and dangerous. They often said things like, "I'm not a label. I'm me." But even with that, I was surprised when in the spring of 2010 a class exercise revealed that one student couldn't even think of herself in terms of identity labels. In conjunction with reading Jewelle Gomez' essay "The Event of Becoming," which distinguishes between reductive and constructive approaches to identity, I asked students to write down the five most salient aspects of their identity on that day, stressing that this was a private exercise and they would not be asked to share their responses. Two days later, I was startled to read in the journal of one of the brightest students in the class that the exercise had spawned a kind of "identity crisis" in her, because she couldn't think of five identity categories for herself. She even went home and discussed it with her roommate, who had the same response.

This was for me a powerful example of one of the things I learn through engagement with my students—that in some ways we do not live in the same world. It was a demonstration of the theories we had been reading—that, indeed, our identities (or even the possibilities of identity) are socially constructed, dependent on historical and material circumstances. As this student and I faced each other across our "gap in experience" (Warland), I realized that my coming out was not enough. I had to continue to find ways to explore the complexities and importance of identity politics with students. It brought to the forefront my worries that in rejecting identity politics, we may indeed only be on TV.

My feelings when I realized how many students were rejecting identity labels were similar to those expressed by Deborah Yaffe in an issue of the on-line lesbian journal *Trivia* tellingly entitled "Are Lesbians Going Extinct?" While being clear that "younger dykes or otherwise queer-identified people have to envision the changes they need from their own experiences," she was still caught off-guard by the new reality:

> . . . I never thought I'd see the day masses of women I think of as lesbians or dykes wouldn't be caught dead wearing the label. What for me was a lifeline to a wider, brighter, more meaningful world is for them a conservative (that is, middle-class, transphobic and dedicated to policing essentialist boundaries), boring, meaningless straightjacket.

I too believe that each generation must have its own language and ways of being in the world that are necessarily different from the generation before. After all, my generation proudly claimed "lesbian" in defiance of a society that had long denied women's sexuality and in rejection of a "gay" identity connected to a sexist political movement.[3]

For all of our differences, I feel privileged to work with students of the current generation, whom I find energetic, hopeful, and technologically sophisticated. I am moved daily by students' passion to change the world, their commitment to social justice and equality. I feel this even when I acknowledge their right to do things their own way and feel confused and hurt by what feels sometimes like rejection. Elana Dykewomon writes powerfully about her experience in this regard:

One minute we were the movement: we were in the middle of it, struggling, yelling, creating, singing, making love . . . and the next moment we were your mother's feminism, absurd, too-sober separatists whose essentialism was holding up the next great push for rights and couldn't we just get out of the way. At least, that's how we often feel about it.

Still, as Dykewomon also writes, when she feels that the "new definitions parse me out of existence . . . it's my job to re-enter the conversation." I agree. By being out, by claiming the identity of lesbian, by teaching lesbian herstory, by listening to my students and asking them to listen to me, we can use our differences for our common work rather than have them silence or divide us. As Audre Lorde wrote about the silence around race within her "gay girl" community in the 1950s: "We were too afraid those differences might in fact be irreconcilable, for we had never been taught any tools for dealing with them" (*Zami* 205). I would say that the tools for dealing with difference are still not commonly known or used; those who don't want us to work together have a great stake in keeping them so.

To work across differences necessitates not a rejection of identity labels, but using them to identify ourselves in all our multiplicity, for that multiplicity within us is a tool for working across differences, and one which should be accessible to all of us. As Audre Lorde said in her commencement speech at Oberlin in 1989:

There will always be someone begging you to isolate one piece of yourself, one segment of your identity above the others and say, "Here, this is who I am." Resist that trivialization. I am not *just* a lesbian. I am not *just* a poet. I am not *just* a mother. Honor the complexity of your vision and yourselves. We

> learn to use each other's differences as creative tools for change by learning
> how to acknowledge and orchestrate the conflicting parts within ourselves,
> learning how to integrate the many different pieces of our identity into action
> behind our beliefs. ("Survival" 12)

It is no accident that lesbians of color have reminded us of the importance of claiming our identities over and over again. In 1977, the Combahee River Collective wrote that as Black women, "We believe that the most profound and potentially the most radical politics come directly out of our own identity" (212). In her introduction to the 1978 edition of *Movement in Black*, Judy Grahn quoted Black lesbian poet Pat Parker as saying, "The day all the different parts of me can come along, we would have what I would call a revolution" (11).

In my Lesbian Literature class in the spring of 2010, the students who did speak up about the power and importance of labels were primarily students of color or student with other non-majority identities and this is something that we cannot ignore. I fear that an interpretation of postmodernism's ideas about the malleability of identity which rejects all labels and assumes that in doing so we are inclusive of everyone's right to be who they are is just another iteration of the lack of analysis of privilege which supports the mainstream. I worry that a postmodern haze has fallen over the discussions of difference and privilege that were an ongoing part of the lesbian feminism communities of which I was a part.

In the last few years, some academics have been severely critical of coming out in class, seeing it as promoting a retrograde essentialism.[4] Yet their notion of coming out seems monolithic and a-contextual. For me coming out is not an announcement on the first day of class, but a process which takes place in the context of a feminist pedagogy in which, in spite of the structural hierarchy in which we do our work together, I encourage a community in the classroom where each person is encouraged to bring her multifaceted self, Pat Parker's idea of a "revolution." While the idea that one even has a self, or parts of a self to bring, has been discredited by postmodern and queer theorists, students by and large respond to this call to community as a place where they can express ideas or tell of past experiences that are not welcome in other places.

I come out to my students in a letter, telling them about the parts of my life I want to share—that I'm from NJ, that I'm Italian American, that my mother died after living with Parkinson's disease for twenty years, that I love the outdoors, that I'm a birdwatcher, that my partner and I have been together for twenty-two years, that she uses a wheelchair, that we built an accessible house. I ask the students to write me a letter of introduction with the heading "Here's what I want you to know about me." This becomes the bedrock for the work we do together.

I make it an overt goal of the class to learn each other's names and to recognize individuals for the experience and knowledge they bring to the discussions. Each student writes a reading journal each week to which I respond in writing, in the form of a letter, which provides an ongoing private discussion that supplements the public one of the class. Each class period we do some kind of exercise that gives each student a chance to participate. Sometimes this is small group work where the instructions call for each person in the group to speak. At other times, we each choose a passage to read aloud, or we do a round robin in which each person responds to the reading for the day, uninterrupted and without comment until all have spoken. Sometimes students prepare a group performance of a poem or do a role-play. Students consistently respond in a positive way to this aspect of the class, writing on evaluations that they appreciated hearing a diversity of viewpoints, they felt heard and respected by others, and they felt part of a community. It's gratifying that students so often mention that they found the class so diverse, because often on the surface, with so little racial diversity in Nebraska, this is not obvious on the first day. Privilege and lack of privilege also become revealed in these class interactions, as we realize how our backgrounds affect our readings of the literature.

To me, these elements of feminist pedagogy are some of the tools we need to explore and use difference and privilege in positive ways. As Audre Lorde said, "We do not need to become each other in order to work together. But we do need to recognize each other, our differences as well as the sameness of our goals" ("Survival" 5). Each year when I approach teaching lesbian feminism in my Lesbian Lit course, I get a knot in my stomach, because in the past several years I have found that most students reject outright the ideas in the Radicalesbians' "Woman Identified Woman" and Adrienne Rich's "Compulsory Heterosexuality." They are so removed from the time period in which these were written and so used to hearing that we all need to work together, that anger is detrimental, and so on, that they cannot hear what these authors are saying. This semester, though, I remembered a useful tool in dealing with difference that I learned in the 1980s in a Women Against Racism Conference called the "Fishbowl." At the conference, women of color took the stage to tell white women what their experience was like, including what they never wanted to hear again and what they wanted from us as allies. We could respond only with "What I heard you say was . . ." and would be shut down if we started to interpret what we understood. In class, we put the authors of our readings in the center of the fishbowl, to tell us how the world looked from their points of view, and, again, the only way we could respond was by saying, "What I heard the author say was . . .," with no interpretation allowed. When the students listened to the authors rather than responding immediately out of their own contexts, they heard so much more. And they found some connections. This is just one example of how we can use tools for analyzing difference and privilege in class in order to break through the surface of "we're all human beings and labels just divide us."

I came out into a vibrant lesbian feminist community in Lincoln, Nebraska in the late 1970s. During that time the local grassroots group the Lincoln Legion of Lesbians held all-women dances, brought lesbian performers to town, met with officials to talk about political and legal issues, and served as a network of information and connection. For several years we had a women's bookstore and for over a decade a feminist newspaper. We have none of these things now. My students don't have this experience—neither the lesbian feminist creations nor the loss of them, but it's exhilarating to tell them what it was like for me, and to hear about what it's like for them, how they are re-envisioning the world. I will continue to come out in class as a lesbian, and I will continue to ask them how they think and talk about their identities.

Notes

1. Holly Near's coming-out album "Imagine My Surprise" was a touchstone for many lesbian feminists of my generation. Significantly for my argument in this essay, Near explains in the liner notes that the "surprise" was both personal and political/historical: "I read this book called *Women Remembered* put out by Diana Press. It was about these poets and pirates who were woman identified. History books did it again . . . forgot to tell us the truth!"
2. In "The Transformation of Silence Into Language and Action," Lorde writes of herself as "a Black woman warrior poet doing my work—come to ask you, are you doing yours?" (41–42). Although I never met Audre Lorde, I felt accountable to her. I wanted to be able to answer her question in the affirmative: "Yes, I am doing my work."
3. In my Lesbian Literature class, we read Lillian Faderman's *Odd Girls and Twilight Lovers: A History of Lesbian Life in Twentieth-Century America* (NY: Penguin, 1991),

in which she examines love between women from a social constructionist stance, based on the understanding that "history does not repeat itself" (4). The book convincingly demonstrates that people language, sexual behaviors, and even concepts about sexuality are shaped by societal factors.

4.   Susan Talburt, *Subject to Identity* (Albany NY: SUNY P, 2000); Karen Kopelson, "Dis/Integrating the Gay/Queer Binary: 'Reconstructed Identity Politics' for a Performative Pedagogy," *College English* 65:1 (2000): 17-35; "Rhetoric on the Edge of Cunning; Or, the Performance of Neutrality (Re)Considered As a Composition Pedagogy for Student Resistance," *CCC* 55:1 (2003): 115-46; and Michelle Gibson, Martha Marinara and Deborah Meem, "Bi, Butch, and Bar Dyke: Pedagogical Performances of Class, Gender, and Sexuality," *CCC* 52:1 (2000): 69–95.

Works Cited

Atwood, Margaret. "An End to Audience?" *Second Words: Selected Critical Prose*. Boston: Beacon P, 1982. 334–357.

Combahee River Collective. "A Black Feminist Statement." *This Bridge Called My Back: Writings by Radical Women of Color*. Ed. Cherrie Moraga and Gloria Anzaldua, NY: Kitchen Table Women of Color Press, 1981. 210–18.

DiBernard, Barbara. "Being an I-Witness: My Life as a Lesbian Teacher." *Private Voices, Public Lives: Women Speak on the Literary Life*. Ed. Nancy Owen Nelson. Denton, TX: U of North TX Press, 1995. 99–110.

Dykewomon, Elana. "Who Says We're Extinct?" *Trivia: Voices of Feminism* 10 (2010): n. pag. Web. 10 April 2010.

Gomez, Jewelle. "The Event of Becoming." *A Queer World*. Ed. Martin Duberman. NY: NYU Press, 1997. 17–23.

Grahn, Judy. Introduction. *Movement in Black*. By Pat Parker. Ithaca, NY: Firebrand, 1978. 11–13.

Lorde, Audre. "A Question of Survival." *Gay Community News* Aug. 13-19 1989: 5, 12. ---. "The Transformation of Silence Into Language and Action." *Sister Outsider*. Trumansburg, NY: Crossing Press, 1984. 40–44. ---. *Zami: A New Spelling of My Name*. 1982. Freedom, CA: Crossing Press, 1997.

Near, Holly. *Imagine My Surprise!* Redwood Records, 1978. Album.

Sturgis, Susanna J. "And Will Rise? Notes on Lesbian Extinction." *Trivia: Voices of Feminism* 10 (2010): n. pag. Web. 10 April 2010.

Warland, Betsy. "Editorial." *Trivia: Voices of Feminism* 10 (2010): n. pag. Web. 10 April 2010.

Yaffe, Deborah. "My Mid-term Exam in Lesbian Theory and Practice: Discuss the question, 'Are Lesbians Going Extinct?' as if your life depended on it." *Trivia: Voices of Feminism* 10 (2010): n. pag. Web. 10 April 2010.

Definition
Sandra Woodson

ℂℌ

The death of dogma is the birth of morality.

—Immanuel Kant

In spring of 2005, the Director of Human Resources and a notary came to a faculty meeting to gather the signature of each faculty member on a "loyalty oath." A dozen or so faculty sat around the large conference table, frowning, looking at each other, at our division director, at the human resources guy. I stared at the oath, a seemingly innocuous series of words:

"I (insert name) hereby swear to uphold the Constitution of the State of Colorado and the Constitution of United States of America." Underneath that sentence was a line to sign and date the oath, and room for the notary to affix her stamp.

To my knowledge, I have never done anything unconstitutional. I tapped my memory for contents of the Constitution. From my repository of School House Rock facts, I recall how the U.S. Constitution includes how a Bill becomes a law, the minimum age of the president, and the separation of powers. There are all the Amendments, but I felt confident that I would never infringe on them.

The Colorado State constitution, on the other hand, is a massive document, over 700 pages I'm told. It's so enormous because it can be amended with a simple majority vote from Colorado citizens, which happens every election cycle. It's hard to keep track. Even so, I'm unclear about how being a lecturer of philosophy at a small engineering college could lead to doing something unconstitutional. So at first blush, the oath seemed pretty safe. Insulting, but safe.

Colorado, however, like many states in the U.S., has had a history of attempts to put a Defense of Marriage Act into its state constitution, and it occurred to me that I might have a problem with that if/when it passed. I was in love with a woman and wanted to marry her. We were talking about going to British Columbia to have our wedding, and I was going to have a document—a marriage license—that might be "unconstitutional." I worried that my intention of sidestepping a law that might end up in the state constitution might be in violation of that stupid oath. I started getting mad. What does this have to do with my teaching?

Our Director of Human Resources said, "If you don't sign it, you'll be fired. If you write 'under duress' beneath your signature, we'll tear it up and try again." I looked around the room and some of my colleagues looked confused, and some were obviously pissed. I teach in a liberal arts department, so I was surrounded by literature professors, historians, a sociologist, the philosophers. "This *is* 'under duress' since we'll lose our jobs if we don't sign it," one professor said.

The Human Resources Man backpedaled a bit and tried to explain how this law had been on the books for decades—since the McCarthy era—and somehow that was supposed to make us all feel better about it. Great. McCarthy. But our governor was adamant about having all faculty in state supported public colleges sign this oath. I'm guessing this was his response the whole liberal-college-faculty-are-indoctrinating-our-most-impressionable-youth thing.

Human Resources Man seemed genuinely surprised by our resistance. He'd been to other departments, and apparently had no problems. I stared at him, tears welling up, frowning. I stared back at the piece of paper. I debated not signing it, about getting fired, about how I'd tell my partner I lost my job because I wouldn't sign a piece of paper, how I wouldn't be able to work at any public university in Colorado because they were all requiring it. I would lose my job for a principle, which sounds sexy at some level, but poverty/stress/anxiety are not fun, states I tried to leave behind after graduate school.

I signed the oath. I didn't even try to write "under duress," I guess because I was powerless to change any of it.

Here's the irony.

I teach ethics, both "regular" ethics and environmental ethics. I tell stories to my students to show how philosophy actually is relevant to their lives. I talk about my dog Daisy and how Kant wouldn't give a fig about her happiness or pain because she's not a rational agent. John Stuart Mill would care though, because she can suffer and suffering is a thing generally to be avoided. I tell stories about my cat Mr. Pancakes who likes to eat the heads off of squirrels and leave the rest of the corpse in the yard in obstacle course fashion. I have to be very careful when I mow the lawn, because if I ever run over one of the headless squirrels, that very well might be the end of me. I tell them that even though I yell at Mr. Pancakes when he does these things (Mister *Pan*cakes!), I don't think he's immoral, of course. He's a cat. He hunts. He eats parts of the things he kills. He is not, I tell them, a moral agent. I tell stories about students who have cheated on tests, about how pissed off I get at drivers on the interstate, about my bartending days. I refer to my partner—my wife—as my "main squeeze." "Partner" is code for same-sex partner, so I avoid using it. "Friend" can be useful—I use that term with my mother's neighbors and distant relatives—but in all my stories for my classes I am very, very careful. These kids are smart.

Part of my story repertoire includes references to old boyfriends. There was, in fact, an Iranian fiancé, when I was 18 and very rebellious. It was 1980, and the Iranian Hostage Crisis was in full bloom. Just the year before—when I was in high school—I had been a part of a group that burned the Ayatollah Khomeini in effigy. I wrote an editorial for the high school newspaper chastising President Carter for being "soft" on terrorists. "Look," I say to my students, "people change. When I was a kid I believed what my parents believed. When I went to college, I started thinking for myself. That's what college is about."

The story is entirely true—I really was engaged to an Iranian back in the day—but there's a part of me that uses it for another code. *Hey. I've had boyfriends. You may think I'm a dyke, but don't be too sure.* I prefer to think I'm oh-so-subtly challenging their assumptions about appearances: I wear jeans, corduroy sport coats, hiking boots. My hair is short, and I wear no makeup, little jewelry. Classic lesbian. Also, classic philosopher. It's important to me that they look beyond appearances and get to content. That is, really, philosophy.

But there's more, and I'm not proud of it: I breathe a little easier thinking the story about the fiancé or other boyfriends might muddy the water of speculation about my orientation. *Oh. Okay. If she had a fiancé, she must be straight. Right?* The college where I work can—by state law—fire me without cause, and being gay is not a protected class like race, religion or ethnicity is. Very concretely, I can be fired for being a lesbian, if higher-ups at my institution decide they don't want my kind here.

One day at the beginning of class, while I was setting up my PowerPoint and putting on my teaching game face, this big, goofy boy said, "Sandy, what does your husband do?" I looked down at my wedding ring. Most of the rest of the class was chatting with each other, but three or four other students were listening to his question, and waiting for my answer.

It's the pronouns that get you.
    Stinking pronouns.
    This is an ethics class.
    I don't want to lie to an *ethics* class, for god's sake.
    I can get fired for being a lesbian.

"He works at DU," I say to the blackboard. I turn to the class and start lecturing on Kant.

"Kant," I tell them, "is completely into rationality. He also has an inordinately large forehead," I say, pointing to an image of him on the screen. "Kant thinks that behaving immorally is fundamentally *irrational*. He even said that 'Lying obliterates the dignity of a human being.' Using our rationality is what makes us human, what sets us apart from other animals. So if we lie, we're sub-human." Kant is *hard*, I tell them, but try. He's one of the smartest people who ever lived. "Once you know Kant's ideas, you'll see them everywhere," I say.

"We've been looking at Mill and Utilitarianism, which is easy. That one is about maximizing happiness, the greatest good for the greatest number. Those ideas aren't alien or crazy to you. Kant, though, is going to say pretty much just the opposite. For him, happiness is not a moral issue."

"I cannot emphasize this enough," I continue. "It's not about consequences for Kant, whether the outcome is good or bad. It's all about using your brain to figure out the right thing to do, and the right thing has absolutely nothing to do with consequences. It all revolves around his idea of a *good will*, acting from rationality."

After class I seek out another professor who teaches ethics and pour out the torrid tale of my lie and betrayal of my dear students, the awful irony of teaching Kant of all philosophers right after this lie, my first overt lie to them, the others were all lies of omission or deflection, but this one, *this one* was a bald-face, full-bore, to-your-face fabrication, entirely intentional, so much worse for the intention. Kant, I know, would be horrified.

I wonder aloud whether maybe I'm selling my students short, maybe they wouldn't care anyway, I bet a lot of them "know" already, even with my evasions. Would some care? Maybe. Maybe they'd shut down, never hear me again, and they wouldn't be able to get past it. They'd only see a big ol' lesbian, dissecting every sentence for "gay mafia indoctrination" instead of learning philosophy. *That* hardly makes for good teaching. In fact, they might tell their parents who might then freak out completely and call the president of the school. Our president is not exactly Mr. Progressive. They could simply not renew my contract. I could lose this job I love.

"Oh, don't worry about it," my colleague said. "It's like Santa Claus. You don't tell kids that Santa doesn't exist because they couldn't handle it."

Santa Claus? Really?

"But I *lied*," I say. "I lied to an ethics class. That is so *wrong*."

Part of my job as a teacher is to model academic behavior. I model respect in the classroom. I model silliness, but also seriousness. I show them just by my existence that women do philosophy, teach college. I model what philosophy is, what philosophers do. Right? *Right?*

The other professor awkwardly pats my shoulder. "Really, it's okay. It's not a big deal." I think he very badly wants me to stop crying. I also think he doesn't get it, can't get it. Part of it is philosophical—he's more Aristotlean than Kantian, so an occasional and prudent lie is not the end of the world—but while he might grasp the irony, he doesn't see the tragedy inherent in my conflict. He doesn't see the ragged edges of exhaustion from trying to hide who I am.

I was ostensibly straight for the first 35 years of my life. I dated men, slept with a few. I worked in a bar much of my adult life, and came to love my gay compatriots in the service industry. I became politically liberal, and didn't understand why anyone cared about other people's sexual orientation. If you think sleeping with someone of the same sex is gross, don't do it. Really, it's not complicated.

As a "gay ally," but still a member of the heterosexual class, I had no idea what it means to walk through the world like I do now. I could not know. I was, as Bataille says, like water in water. The operating assumption is that the vast majority of people you meet are hetero— which is statistically correct of course—but I didn't recognize what I see now. Straight people don't have to worry about introducing their spouse, referring to their spouse as he or she, wonder whether anyone caught the casual, intimate "honey," that slipped out in mixed company. What I didn't understand, most of all I think, is the relentless question about whether I ought to correct that assumption of heterosexuality.

Adrienne Rich: A half-truth is a whole lie.

Yes, I'm married, but to a woman.

She works at DU.

She's a poet.

My wife…

If allowing people to go on believing that I'm hetero is a lie, I lie every day. The Kantian in me shrinks in horror, recoils at the prospect of my abdicating my humanity. My utilitarian bits try to weigh my discomfort and fear against that of my students'. Aristotle, gives me the most hope and murkiness of all: he would probably be perfectly fine with my attempt at balancing the virtues of dignity, courage and forth-rightness, but he would also challenge me to be a good person, to live a good life. He would most explicitly challenge me to model the good life for my students. As much as I know about ethics, about some of the greatest thinkers in the western tradition, I still don't know what I should do.

I know as a teacher I have to establish all sorts of boundaries with my students. I am not their friend, even as I'm friendly to them and genuinely like them. Even if I didn't have a wife, there would be whole constellations of stories that would be off-limits. My nagging question is where my orientation fits in with my teaching life. Teaching, it seems to me, is more than explaining theory; teaching is *living a life*. My life, my very existence as a lesbian, is a challenge to some students—an important challenge—that I bury. That I could and should be a role model for GLBT students at this small, conservative college gnaws at me. I worry that I'm doing a disservice to myself, my students, my partner, and my institution.

Some days, I wish I had refused to sign the oath, been fired, but had stood up for my convictions. Many days I wish had the courage to simply refer to my wife as my wife, and stop worrying about consequences. But teaching is all about consequences. So instead, when students ask me whether I'm "Mrs. or Miss," I tell them to call me "Professor," and I continue to live in a realm of blurry edges and half-truths, where Kant and Mill and Aristotle vie for my allegiance, and perpetuate a lie.

Playing With Gender for College Credit: *Experiencing Gender, Sex and Sexuality*
Anne Balay

☙

Often, after taking my *Women's and Gender Studies 201: Gender in Everyday Life* course for a month or two, students complain that I have ruined their lives. They can no longer view anything in the same way. Everything they experience in the world, in their other courses, and in their daily lives comes under critique. As they themselves put it, they can no longer have fun. Movies make them angry, rather than relaxed. Their parents, partners, children, bosses, even friends, make uneven demands, and don't seem to even want to change their ways. The government and society just go on doing the unfair, illogical things they have been doing all along. Identifying inequality, and how ingrained it is in every level of our daily lives, feels transformative and empowering, but it also feels claustrophobic and entrapping, since it is so resistant to change on the psycho-personal level, as well as the macro-political level, and everywhere in between. Though these students are genuinely unhappy, they are usually not sorry to have taken the class. Seeing problems, sharing them with others, and trying to envision solutions or improvements, feel like important steps to them, and their distress indicates that education is occurring.

Further, the class's irritation, fully shared by its instructor, is directed inward as well as outward. We are mad at ourselves and struggle to bring about personal change. For example, we notice how, as women, we habitually say "sorry" when people bump into us, whether or not we are responsible. Automatically, we smile, or otherwise placate others to avoid conflict, or the perception of hostility. When pressed, we often don't know what we "want," since we are so focused on pleasing others. One goal of the class, then, is to interrogate these levels of discomfort, working towards some sense of what to change, and how. Just as feminist theory insists on the bi-directional claim that "the personal is political," I believe that feminist pedagogy works best when it enacts the relationship between personal experience and course content as a reciprocal exchange. That is, students and teachers bring their varied contexts and experiences into the classroom, never forgetting that knowledge is always structured by gender, race, class, sexuality, age, religion, etc. Simultaneously, students and teachers take the course content out into their lives and other classes.

As Critical Race Feminism (an emerging branch of legal pedagogy) has argued, detachment, value-neutral objectivity, and silence about personal life are tools that facilitate exclusive education by making it invisible (Guinier 108). Within the first week of class, I identify myself as a lesbian, not only as part of a post-Stonewall politics of visibility, but also to open up the question of gender performance. Our region is very conservative—it's a mixture of farms, heavy industry, and those avoiding the urban menace of nearby Chicago. Many of my students have never knowingly met a gay person before. Curiosity is their dominant reaction, and my job at this point is simply to *be*—validating some stereotypes, contradicting others—representing one example of lesbian existence.

The classroom is very diverse, consisting of overlapping groups of queer folks, racial minorities, women with children, and those barely subsisting on the fringes of this bad economy. Early in the class, I merely point to this variety, noting the distance between femininity and heterosexuality, between hard work and financial reward, between race and identity. We spend the bulk of the semester mucking up these waters even further. A feminist pedagogy needs to take the risk of seeming personal, flaky, and unprofessional, because doing so can challenge standards by which only empirical knowledge is valued, and only de-personalized learning is valid. Education then can become hybrid and contingent; something created by students, rather than absorbed by them.

My introductory Women's and Gender Studies course hinges on assignments and exercises that bridge the divide between school and life. I hope to get students excited, involved, and participating, such that the classroom becomes a community, of which the teacher is a member. As bell hooks argues, radical teachers "are not performers in the traditional sense of the word in that our work is not meant to be a spectacle. Yet it is meant to serve as a catalyst that calls everyone to become more and more engaged, to become active participants in learning" (11). It would be easy to dismiss the experiments of my class as more interesting than educational, or more theatric than thoughtful. I have two responses. First, these experiments are only one component of a course that also includes detailed readings of two novels and numerous analytical essays. Second, the distinction between doing and thinking—between brain and body—is one that we question and challenge throughout the course.

We begin with the traditional gender violation exercise pioneered by Jean Fox O'Barr, and practiced in Women's Studies classes for decades. We usually do this experiment during the second week of class, when concepts like gender roles, the multi-valence of oppression and of privilege, and student's names are percolating and becoming familiar.

Students start by listing things they consider inappropriate for their gender. I agree with O'Barr that "[s]tudents know the dominant gender culture and bring it with them to the classroom and the campus where it is reinforced" (126). They have a long and rigid set of rules about what men and women should and should not do. However, O'Barr wrote her essay in the 1990s, though her observation still stands, now students are under more pressure *not* to notice the gender rules and roles that confine them. Many students will proudly claim that, for them, anything is possible, nothing is off-limits, and therefore, this exercise is impossible—a charming tribute to a bygone era. I start by acknowledging that feeling of power and possibility, and filling in some historical background about where it came from and who paid for it. Then, I encourage students to think about the invisible, self-effacing codes and standards they follow, without even noticing they are doing so. I put students in groups for solidarity and support, and have them think about accepted norms for dating, manners, jobs, family life, public behavior, fashion, speech, movement, access to public space, etc. Once they get started, the lists of gender taboos usually accumulate quickly and easily.

Once each student has a list of inappropriate actions, I put students in pairs, and have each pick an action they can do, on campus, in front of the other student. The goal of the exercise is to get students to expand their gender limits and explore the tangled web of shame, embarrassment, fear, and freedom that this entails. O'Barr states that "[o]ur only requirement was that they take along an observer, whose commentary plays an important role in their subsequent analysis of the experiment" (122). Each student in turn becomes the observer/ expert, who reports back to class. Sometimes the observer can note the punitive actions of others, but on other occasions, the observer can prod the violator into reflecting on personal, internalized censure.

The experiment gets students to see gender roles that normally remain invisible. It also encourages students to play with gender—to not take it so seriously, to be wild and laugh and bond. Because gender is a rigidly hierarchical system, from which there is no real escape, the gender violation exercise parallels Bakhtin's idea of carnival, which "celebrated temporary liberation from the prevailing truth and from the established order; it marked the suspension of all hierarchical rank, privileges, norms and prohibitions" (199). Just as carnival depends on a rigid caste system for its meaning, the violation exercise depends on, and does not negate, gender roles. However, it allows the class to notice them, viscerally feel how hard they are to break, and laugh at ourselves and at the system of which we are a part. This process, then, becomes a foundation for thinking about how gender effects our lives, and working out what part of that structure we want to keep, and what we want to reject or modify.

Halfway through semester, we spend a day thinking—as people who have been reading about and living this subject for more than a month—about the things we do because of our gender roles that we wish we didn't. At this moment, course members hear, and share, the stories that hurt. For example, I always pick up after my children and my partner. One year, I had a pattern where I made a smoothie for my elder daughter every day, and she would carry it into her room to finish it after breakfast. Then, before leaving for work, I would go into her room, get the empty glass, rinse it, and put it in the dishwasher. I hated myself for doing this, because I knew it just trained her to assume that I would do it, and therefore not do it herself. But, I did it. Every day. Class members can name anything they do that they don't want to do. For example, purses. Or shaving. Or taking the blame to avoid a conflict. Or doing favors for others. Or not crying or showing feelings. Once we have a good list, we pick three that resonate with the most people. Then, each class member has to choose one of the three, and engage to break their gender rule, whenever possible, for the next six weeks, keeping a journal of what they did and how it felt.

One effect of this exercise is to disrupt the usual power dynamics of the classroom. In this project, we are all designing and doing something hard, and figuring out what it means, together. One student who chose not to carry a purse discussed, both verbally and in writing, how many side effects this change caused in her life. For example, she had small children, and she was the parent who transported the endless extras (pacifiers, diapers, books, comfort objects, extra clothes, etc.) they might need, because she had a handy means by which to do so. This role contributed to her being seen as the parent to go to in distress, and thus became a part of the enforcement of traditional parental roles. As another consequence, her purse was heavy, literally weighing her down and causing back pain. Metaphorically, then, her purse symbolized both the burden of motherhood, and the open-ended availability and emotional sensitivity of the maternal role. Not carrying her purse allowed this student to notice aspects of her life which had been invisible before. Noticing, of course, is not changing. But it is a first step, and it felt very important to this student, and to the class, who helped and supported her through this process of self-discovery.

More pedantically, other students who chose this task were led to ask why women's clothes don't have pockets. The basics of wallet, keys, and cell phone should be stowable on one's person. Does the fashion industry deny this convenience to women on purpose, so that we will then buy purses? So that we will then have to carry an extra burden? To increase our vulnerability to theft, and thereby our fear? Or is it that lumps and bumps in our clothes would take away from the feminine desire to appear smooth and thin at all costs? Key here is that students notice, often for the first time, that garments like blue jeans, which seem fundamentally the same for men and women, are subtly but powerfully different, in ways that effect our gender performance and identity.

The class wants to know how my own experiment is progressing, and they use this to learn more about my life. They know by now that I am a lesbian, forty-six, a mother of teenaged girls, white, non-religious, and an English Professor. And class discussions often involve illustrative stories drawn from my life. This longer gender violation exercise, by giving us all similar problems, involves my personal life and struggles more intimately in class discussion—it takes the feminist commitment to including the personal in class (Stake, hooks, Barone) to a scarier level. For example, last year I decided to refuse to do favors for others, and I totally failed. I had to share with my students how bad

I was at this. My partner works two miles from our house, and I drive very close to her job on the way to my, more distant, workplace. That winter included many cold days, in which she occasionally asked me to drive her, and her bike, to work. I didn't want to. It takes more time and effort than it seems. It's not a big deal, but it *is* just one more thing to deal with. But, I could not say no. My students were incredulous that I even considered saying it. It was *very* cold. Why should she bike? At the same time, I pointed out to them that no one has ever delivered me to my job. Not once in my entire life. Why am I perpetually on the service end of life? Even writing about this now makes me feel whiney and unloving, which I felt then, and incorporated into our class discussion about gender roles.

Ultimately, I had to drop that exercise, and revert to not picking up after others. Though this is challenging and important for me, the class community learned as much from my failure as from my subsequent progress. Especially since another student stuck with the initial scheme, and really blossomed there. She was also a lesbian single mother of one teenaged daughter. Her father kicked her out when she became pregnant in high school, and she has supported herself and the child since then. She did an excellent job raising Susan. To compensate for their isolation and her youth, she was very involved in school, and became the mother who does everything. This without education, resources, or family support. During the course of the gender violation exercise, she came to believe that she was doing too much for her daughter, who was consequently not developing her own resources. She began to say "no," to talk her way through the accusations and emotional fall out, to articulate its impact on her *own* identity, and to grow. Her discussions of this experience, in class and in essays, were magical – the class community was touched and inspired by her progress. It felt like real feminism was happening, and that someone with a GED was more capable than someone with a Ph.D. made it more intense.

The course ends with one final, glorious gender violation exercise. I encourage students to come to school on the last day in drag.

Whatever gender they don't normally present as, they need to try to perform, though not so seamlessly that people don't notice something odd. The goal is to trouble the gender binary, and mobilize laughter that is "gay, triumphant, and at the same time mocking, deriding" (Bakhtin 200). Doing drag, or seeing others do it, brings home lessons about gender and its impact that we have been developing all semester. It is one thing to read that queerness, in addition to being an identity, is also a punitive tool by which any undesirable variation from appropriate gender is proscribed. It's another thing entirely to have this happen to you. This semester, Cassie, who is a pretty, if aggressive freshman with one son, dressed as a sporty, slightly raggedy skater boy. It was good drag. When I passed her on the stairs, even knowing that it was drag day, I didn't recognize her. Yet she reports that across campus and elsewhere, she frequently heard the admonitory slur "dyke." These comments name not a lesbian, but a bad women—someone who fails to get it right. When lesbianism is invisible, it doesn't elicit this pejorative censure, suggesting that sexuality is less the issue than gender roles are.

Steven Schacht invites his students to attend drag shows with him as a means to achieve similar ends. He notes that students readily accept that gender is constructed, but that viewing actual drag queens encourages them to internalize this message on a more visceral level. The students' own actions and reactions at the bar allow them "to experientially challenge their dichotomous, often oppressive, beliefs about the social categories of male and female, gay and straight" (Schacht 227). The point here is that identity and sexuality are not linked to particular bodies (Brueggemann 210). All people tend to experience gander and sexuality as obvious, natural expressions of their bodies ("It's just the way I am"), whereas seeing or doing drag emphasizes that they are arbitrary and changeable ("It's what I'm doing right now"). This spring, the class butch and a mild-mannered straight girl found themselves with the most masculine demeanor and attitude, and unexpectedly enjoyed the edgy, sexy challenge that ensued. Each one instructed the other in masculine movement and occupancy of space in a coolness contest that was both flirtatious and aggressive. Masculinity is not, after all, restricted to men, or even to men and lesbians. As Judith Halberstam explains, "female-born people have been making convincing and powerful assaults on the coherence of male masculinity for well over a hundred years" (15). Observing this type of interaction really shakes something loose in the class community's sense of how gender, sexuality, and the erotic are linked.

As an out lesbian professor, I'm somewhat cautious about introducing eroticism into the classroom, but also conscious of its inevitable, often unacknowledged, presence, *and* excited by its possibility. I'm not "supposed" to be attracted to students, I'm not "supposed" to be attracted to men. As a Professor, my desire, most especially my deviant desire, is foreclosed. But sexuality is messy. The butch and the straight girl liked eachother. I like muscular, masculine women *and* men in drag. Students who had finally gotten comfortable with my "sexual orientation" have to rethink it again, and rethink theirs, too. As Alexander observes, "in marking our sexual orientation, we encourage straight students (and faculty) to mark their sexual orientations and become aware of the ways in which sexuality is labeled, codified, and political in our society" (162) and specifically in our classrooms (173).

The only gay male in class this semester was a quiet, somewhat awkward and self-effacing, bearded, skinny white boy. He had never done drag before, and seemed reluctant because shaving would be required. For maximum impact, he arrived about ten minutes after class began, and the otherwise boisterous room fell immediately silent. He was gorgeous, yes, but he was also an entirely different person. His demeanor sought, and fed on, attention. His very presence shifted the energy of the room.

As a class, we began to explore why. Perhaps gender is a hiding place—we, especially those deviant in some way, have been shamed by and through it for so long that breaking its chains feels glorious. The audience is then responding to that radiance. Or perhaps gender violation is inherently sexy. Brandon's back, arms and shoulders had a masculine musculature certainly not showcased by his usual loose t-shirts, but very apparent in his skimpy black gown. Similarly, many female students, both in and out of drag, observed that their fellow students made very hot boys—different, dangerous, and strangely appealing. We do gender without really thinking about it, but doing it "wrong" also unleashes something powerful and disturbing. We discuss these possibilities in class. We laugh, and squirm, and go home to think about it. I do not offer answers, not only because I don't have them, but also because I want the thinking and asking to continue unchecked in all our minds and lives.

Feminist pedagogy and queer politics infiltrate our lives. They affect what we wear, what we do, and how we do it. This course specifically tries to increase awareness of how gender and sexuality subtly steer us towards certain behaviors and away from others. As one final example, I feel uncomfortable writing an article that is aggressive, confident, and even boastful. I am not uncomfortable talking about my family and my feelings with my students, but I shy away from promoting myself. Being an openly lesbian professor is challenging, and may inhibit my career advancement. Scholars have noted that teaching evaluations influence tenure and promotion decisions, and that out gay and lesbian teachers often get negative comments on these evaluations. University committees may not understand that such comments result from bias and bigotry, and conclude instead that they reflect troubling classroom dynamics. For example, in a class where my being gay came up once, towards the end, when we were reading a Young Adult novel about teenaged lesbians, I got this comment: "was this a children's lit class or an exploration in our homosexuality?" And, more scathingly, for the class discussed in this article, one student noted: "Quit talking about gay/lesbian people just because you are one doesn't mean we have to hear about it every day. A lot of your views are upsetting & you need to consider everyone's own personal ideas & beliefs." Though most students are incredibly enthusiastic, and report transformations of their lives and academic missions, it is these negative comments that reviewers remember. I was turned down for a teaching award this year, and one reason given was hostile teaching evaluations (and, really, I have quoted the only negative comments here). I have been encouraged to avoid applying for tenure based on teaching excellence for this reason as well.

Research demonstrates that students criticize professors who are openly gay, and attribute much more credibility to professors they perceive as straight (Russ). All minority teachers are subject to this type of unacknowledged student prejudice (Russ 318), with gay teachers having the added factor that disclosure is seen as both problematic and voluntary. This situation limits both the careers of out gay faculty and the learning of all students, since educators acknowledge that you learn less from those you distrust.

However, it would be counterproductive to "pander to students' stereotypes" (Russ 322) by remaining closeted in order to help students learn the material, and to increases chances of tenure. Students learn from what we do, as well as what we teach, and for student attitudes about gay professors to change, we have to start somewhere. Therefore, I arrive at work in drag on drag day, I am the faculty advisor for the student gay club, and I come out in any class in which it is remotely relevant. Ironically, gender and sexuality continue to tie me in knots. I have a strong desire to please, and I want students and colleagues to like me. I don't like to brag about my bravery or my radical teaching methods. I'm the sole support of two daughters, which requires me to keep my salary coming. All these are part of my training as a woman. Yet as a lesbian, my visibility, my willingness to take risks, and my sense that I'm entitled to fair play contribute to the process of education. When gender and sexuality overlap, and even contradict each other, there are openings through which we can step. When we see how they limit us, we can find the motivation and the mechanism to begin to change. My class helps its members find those disruptions in the rules and roles of gender and sexuality, and use them to continue the revolution.

Works Cited

Alexander, Jonathan. "A `Sisterly Camaraderie' and Other Queer Friendships: A Gay Teacher Interacting With Straight Students." In The Teacher's Body: Embodiment, Authority and Identity in the Academy. Ed. Diane P. Freedman and Martha Stoddard Holmes. Albany: State U of NY P, 2003: 161–177.

Bakhtin, M. M. The Bakhtin Reader: Selected Writings of Bakhtin, Modvedev, Voloshinov. Ed. Pam Morris. London: Edward Arnold, 1994.

Barrone, Tom. Aesthetics, Politics and Educational Inquiry: Essays and Examples. NY: Peter Lang, 2000.

Brueggemann, Brenda Jo and Debra A. Moddelmog. "Coming Out Pedagogy: Risking Identity in Language and Literature Classrooms." In The Teacher's Body: Embodiment, Authority and Identity in the Academy. Ed. Diane P. Freedman and Martha Stoddard Holmes. Albany: State U of NY P, 2003: 209–233.

Halberstan, Judith. Female Masculinity. Durham, Duke UP, 1998.

hooks, bell. Teaching To Transgress: Education as the Practice of Freedom. NY: Routledge, 1994.

Guinier, Lani. "Of Gentlemen and Role Models." in Critical Race Feminism: A Reader. 2nd Ed., Ed. By Adrien Katherine Wang. NY; New York UP, 2003: 209–225.

O'Barr, Jean Fox. Feminism In Action: Building Institutions & Community Through Women's Studies. Chapel Hill, U of North Carolina P, 1994.

Russ, Travis L., Cheri J. Simonds and Stephen K. Hunt. "Coming Out in the Classroom . . . An Occupational Hazard?: The Influence of Sexual Orientation on Teaching Credibility and Perceived Student Learning." Communication Education 51.3 (July 2002): 311–324.

Schacht, Steven P. "Beyond the Boundaries of the Classroom: Teaching About Gender and Sexuality at a Drag Show." Journal of Homosexuality. 146. ¾ (2004): 225–240.

Stake, Jane. "Pedagogy and Student Change in the Women's and Gender Studies Classroom." Gender and Education. 2006.

What My Women's College Taught Me About Being Enthusiastically Queer

Shannon Weber

ৎ১

When I entered college in the fall of 2005, I began to identify as a lesbian on the ivy-covered campus of Mount Holyoke College in western Massachusetts, the oldest women's college in the United States and an environment saturated with affirmations of queerness. At Mount Holyoke I forged my new identity not in a crucible of self-loathing, crisis, and external hatred so typical of "coming out" narratives, but in a queer-positive and in many ways queer-promoting environment. On campus, being queer is seen as exciting, daring, unspeakably beautiful, and *worth it*, despite what homophobic family members and the world outside the Mount Holyoke "bubble" might have to say.

I know of prominent and popular faculty members who identify within the queer spectrum, and I have some great bonds with a few of them. In fact, when my then-fiancée (another Mount Holyoke student in the same class year) and I eloped to San Francisco one week before Proposition 8 passed in California and missed classes during the most intense and eventful twenty-four hour period of my life, my thesis advisor warmly congratulated me and shared my amazement. My bosses from my two on-campus jobs are lesbians; in fact, my wife and I were invited to the home of one boss and her partner at the end of senior year to share a lovely meal and conversation. This is to say nothing of the incredible population of queer students on campus, from which I have made lasting friendships and incredible memories.

Mount Holyoke's queer-positive environment instilled in me the conviction that queerness is paradoxically both commonplace and magical, something "normal" as well as refreshingly different and worth celebrating. The campus, or "Mohome" as we at Mount Holyoke are fond of calling it, did indeed become my adopted home; in fact, as someone who spent most of her life growing up alienated in Idaho among Republican evangelicals, the welcoming and progressive region of Massachusetts' Pioneer Valley was the first place I felt I truly belonged. It is hard to completely convey the breathless warm glow I felt when I experienced a female *a cappella* rendition of "Every Little Thing She Does is Magic" in the campus center, to wild applause, or the surprising and exhilarating opening up of options I felt when my Hall President, the first day I was at Mount Holyoke, informed dorm members of the rules about letting "your boyfriend or girlfriend" visit the residential halls. Being queer at Mount Holyoke is something simple, obvious, and entrenched, as well as something popular and desirable. Thus, with Mount Holyoke as my home and queer students as my community, I formed an exciting new identity with unshakeable foundations that have served me well in preparing for the inevitable reactions to both my identity and my research interests outside the bubble.

After graduation, my wife and I relocated to the Santa Barbara area of California, where I began graduate school and she took up a job as an elementary school reading tutor (a position fraught with its own special anxieties about homophobia and heterosexism!). While taking the bus home from campus one day, the bus driver, an elderly white male, looked at me and my wife through his mirror and decided to start up a conversation with (only) me. Because it was just the three of us on the bus, it was impossible to avoid the attention. As always occurs, his inquiry about what I study raised pesky knots in my stomach, but as usual, I answered anyway: "Feminist Studies." This was followed by an awkward and all-too-expected conversation about whether I was seeing the "full picture" by only studying women. When I replied that I actually study a wide range of people who often aren't included in the "full picture," namely LGBTQ people, he didn't make a fuss, but it was also doubtful whether he understood the alphabet soup acronym that has such personal meaning in my life.

The bus driver's questions were yet another reminder that my association with "Feminist Studies" is only the tip of the iceberg in terms of the frantic uneasiness that heteronormative, at best, and heterosexist, at worst, people will greet me with when they learn of my profession.

The fact that I study queer studies, and that I am by proxy closely linked with queerness, indeed identify as lesbian, makes a seemingly-innocuous bit of small talk balloon into all sorts of personal politics that go beyond even the stigmatized label of "feminism." When my colleagues affiliated with Feminist Studies share their uncomfortable experiences explaining their departmental affiliations outside academia, or even within academic departments less hospitable to feminism, it still seems somehow one degree removed from the situations that ensue when those queer-identified of us in LGBTQ studies suddenly find not only our political beliefs, but our *personal lives* up for scrutiny by those for whom "gay" is an even bigger anathema than "feminism."

I am fully aware that feminism and feminists are still widely disparaged, mocked, and reviled—I am, after all, in Feminist Studies. I do not find "oppression Olympics" very fruitful as a general rubric in determining who can lay claim to the most marginalized experience; we all are affected by power, privilege and oppression in different and overlapping ways. However, I would like to highlight the dilemmas faced by those of us in academia for whom our connection to feminism is not the most controversial or socially condemned part of our identities as scholars or, indeed, as people in general. In short, when I say I'm in Feminist Studies to a skeptical, elderly white male, that's the easy version of what I'm about.

Because of my location as a queer woman steeped in radical politics who cares about what is going on in the streets as well as the journals, I believe strongly in queer visibility and advocacy. I don't personally believe in remaining silent, whenever it's safe to speak up, although I have more than once in the past and must continually negotiate and fight for the courage to truthfully represent my life. I am sometimes tempted, of course, to take an easy way out, even if it is to answer "Women's Studies" to a skeptical and conservative inquirer rather than "Feminist Studies." But I know only too well the stakes involved in this type of mincing of words: if I can't even articulate my field of study, then I *surely* can't talk about anything queer, and by proxy, I can't mention most meaningful aspects of my life. To stifle my response about my work might as well be the same as omitting relevant information about the fact that I'm married to a woman and the dozens of little details that come up as heterosexual people unselfconsciously refer to their different-sex partners in the everyday vignettes that arise in any given conversation. Unless I am facing a life-threatening situation, to erase my wife's existence from my life in order to make some heterosexual people more comfortable is not an option.

Within academia, then, I have been privileged both in belonging
to a field that is actively queer-positive as well as coming from an
environment in which I was never made to feel that being queer is
anything less than amazing. As a white woman, I also do not face the
same pressures and obstacles that my queer female colleagues of color
must daily navigate, and my positionality as cisgender and able-bodied
further contribute to the ways I benefit from hegemonic hierarchies
both within and outside academia. Because of my scholarly focus in
queer studies, however, my own connection to queerness comes up in
even more contexts than it might otherwise (which is also connected
to the fact that I do not visually present as "dykey," which has its own
privileges and drawbacks).

Nonetheless, in articulating "the classroom" as a safe space for
queerness, I sometimes feel hesitant about how much of my personal
life, and my queerness, should come up in the classroom. I fear that at
least some measure of my anxiety is related to a lurking fear of others'
homophobia even as I am a teaching assistant for courses with heavily
queer content. Thankfully my first teaching assistantship experience,
for the class "Sex, Love and Romance," was with a queer role model
of an instructor who herself identifies as a lesbian and who matter-
of-factly, and humorously, mentioned her own relationship with her
wife to students more than once during the course of the class. Her
anecdotes were charming and graceful, reminiscent of something Ellen
DeGeneres would quip about Portia on her talk show. Even so, by the
very nature of living in the United States as part of a same-sex couple,
particularly being married in California amidst the continued legal
battle over Proposition 8, the instructor's stories had to be purposive
and self-conscious. When she mentioned her wife to the class with a
smile and a laugh, I wondered how long it would take for those of us in
same-sex relationships to stop feeling that breathless crevice of fear that
continues to slip in despite our best intentions and our most prideful
identities. This is also to say nothing of the numerous states in which
it is still legal to fire individuals for being queer, and the even larger
number of states in which employers are permitted to fire transgender
and gender-nonconforming individuals.

I felt this crevice of fear when I taught students about violence
against queer people, particularly transgender people and butch
women during pre-Stonewall police raids, and about the restrictive laws
that punished individuals who did not have on at least three articles of
"gender-appropriate" clothing. I wondered, should I somehow work

my own queer identity into this discussion? It's not quite about *me*—but then it sort of is. I faced the same question when I responded to a student's comment that the "Don't Ask Don't Tell" policy is legitimate because it keeps what should be private, private. After letting other students chime in—all of whom were passionately against the policy—I explained that U.S. soldiers are unable to speak about their families, unable to write and receive love letters, unable to talk on the phone to their significant others without fear of discharge, and that spouses and partners of gay soldiers effectively are not allowed to *exist*, including receiving any types of benefits or even know that their loved one has been injured or killed. During this discussion, I thought, should I insert my own life into this? I have never been in the military, but as a lesbian, should I make the immediacy of the situation real by using myself as a hypothetical example? I opted to give an example of my lesbian friend in the Marines, wondering all the time if I was trying to let the students in on my gayness at an irrelevant juncture or whether I was actually giving in to the fear of being viewed as deviant.

Despite these challenges, as I review what it means to be queer in the classroom and how my own experiences of becoming a queer women's college student and alumna compare with those of my LGBTQ colleagues, I am continually struck by the sad marginality of my own relatively positive experiences. Due mostly to the incredible privilege and good fortune I have had as someone who identified as straight throughout high school and who was thus able to emerge unscathed from the likely hell of identifying as queer at my northern Idaho high school; someone who has a supportive family; and as a woman who attended one of the most gay-friendly American liberal arts colleges, my induction into the world of queerness was one of unbounded and joyous potentiality. I studied queer topics in the classroom, and sexual diversity was treated with respect by educators and students alike, although transgender, racial, and class issues all unfortunately remain to be adequately dealt with at Mount Holyoke. In terms of being a lesbian, however, I did not have to "come out" from a dark and shadowy closet but rather realized my potential and joined a fantastic party. The fact that this experience sounds so unbelievable to those outside it is symptomatic of the pervasive heterosexism and homophobia that creep into American living rooms and classrooms alike. Continually reasserting my presence in academia without shame, which is to include my research in LGBTQ studies and the reality of my own queer positionality in addition to the fact that my degree-in-progress is in Feminist Studies, is to pay homage to my proud queer origins.

At the end of our "Sex, Love and Romance" course, the instructor gave students the option to e-mail her a photo of themselves with someone they loved, whether romantically or platonically, which she would then compile into a slideshow for the last day of class. She e-mailed me individually to ask me if I would submit some of my wedding photos. I did so gladly, excited that I was able to participate with her in a unified front of academics with same-sex spouses. I found it important for the straight students in the class to understand that the queer people, cultures, and history they had read about were and are concrete, living and breathing, and all around them. Despite my little knot of fear about being "othered" by the students' gaze and the very mild embarrassment of having my sentimental "personal moments" staring into my wife's eyes in pure bliss blown up to giant proportions on a classroom projector, I truly enjoyed the *legitimating* of that moment, that yes, I am your teaching assistant and this is the woman I love. The compliments from awed students as they left class, particularly about how beautiful our dresses were, were a perfect end to a lovely class that gives me hope for my generation as well as my ability to stay true to the joyously queer identity that Mount Holyoke cultivated in me over the course of four too-short years in New England.

Teacher Coming Out to Teachers
Mary Clare Powell

❧

"Hi," I say. "I'm your poetry teacher, Mary Clare, and I'm eager to get to know you and work with you as you enter the world of poetry." I am in Kent, Washington, in 1995 to teach teachers how to integrate poetry into their curricula and before that, to help them feel comfortable in the house of poetry. To experience themselves as readers and writers of poetry, to re-claim poetry as something they enjoyed.

"Before I say one more word, or you do," I go on, "before we speak of poetry, I invite you to write a short poem about you and poetry. It's called an acrostic." They lie out the letters of their name down the left side of the page and plunge in. After we share some of these, they tell me who they are and I introduce myself to them, show them the poetry books I've written, and talk about my work as a poet. I never say the word "lesbian," but I do say I have a partner for the last twenty-five years, and after that I use the pronoun "she" as referring to the partner. Later I refer to stepchildren and grandchildren. I leave it to them to figure out who I am. She who has ears to hear, let her hear. When we do an exercise involving making metaphors about our families, I begin by having us bring and lay down on the floor pictures of who our families are. I lay down my partner, grandchildren and children. Unknown to me, an older woman in the course flinches when she figures out who I am. She doesn't say anything to me, but begins to speak to all the students in little groups throughout the first weekend: "I think she is a lesbian; I think she's gay."

As we went through the first weekend, I felt them draw back from me—most of them anyway. They resisted my ideas and my prompts for poems and they whispered as I talked. We had started out on one footing and were now on another, and I was baffled. After a month I returned for the second and concluding weekend of the course. I found them dutiful but dispirited, not eager to try things I suggested, almost bored. I soldiered on, knowing I was a good teacher—fair and personable, smart, creative, eager to support everyone's jump into poetry. At home after the second weekend, I knew something hadn't gone well, but didn't know what. My evaluations were lousy when I thought I'd done a good job.

I teach in the Creative Arts in Learning Program at Lesley University in Cambridge, Massachusetts. Lesley has pioneered cohort learning in an off campus model, which offers Master's degrees to teachers in integrating the arts into whatever curriculum they are teaching. The courses are intensive instruction bundled into two full weekends a month apart. The faculty is the outsider, and the students know each other very well, experiencing births, divorces, and marriages, and all the trials of the teaching life—together. When a new faculty member comes, her first work is to be known by them and to begin to know them.

When I started at Lesley University in 1992, I had been "out" for thirty years, and was a poet, but a newcomer to academia. I knew that it was important for me to be truthful with my students about who I was, yet I didn't want to provoke their prejudice or outrage. I knew that coming out would create space for those students who might need to come out as gay or any other hidden minority. At Lesley, I heard that our students would probably be more conservative than we were and that we weren't to bring East Coast liberalism to the heartland. I listened to the talk and still knew that I must come out, one way or another. I also knew from life experience that this knowledge could derail a class. But, I thought surely to be true education, we all had to have a certain measure of trust and honesty. I intended to name myself lesbian.

A year after the Kent Poetry course was over, I taught at a symposium on multicultural education and the arts held for all our cohorts in western Washington. There were eight faculty members there, and about three hundred students. One day, the same student, I'll call her Sue, came up to me as I was speaking with the Dean. She asked for a moment with me, and to my astonishment, told me that she owed me a great apology. "I judged you," she said. "I was afraid of you because my fifty-year old sister just told my parents and me that she is gay. It just about destroyed my father, and my whole family, which had been so close, and we were torn apart, warring, and fearful and anguished. It was too much, you being gay as well." And then she continued: "I undermined our whole poetry course, and I know I changed the tone of our class. I told everyone you were a lesbian, and some people didn't want to have anything to do with you after that. Now I'm a recovering alcoholic and working the twelve steps, and I'll do whatever I can to make it up to you. It was my own fear that I was afraid of, my own ignorance, my own hurt about my sister."

I stood perfectly still and looked into her face. Tears filled my eyes. I said, "See that woman over there?" I pointed to the Dean. "One thing you could do is to explain to her what happened in our class, since she called me in about my evaluations. 'What in the world did you do to provoke that rating?' she asked. You could tell her what you did when you found out I was a lesbian." And she did. I asked about her sister and we talked about what to say to her family, and how to come to terms with her own fears. At the end of our talk, I hugged her.

A few months later she called me. "How far do you live from Boston?" she asked. "My friend and I are coming to Boston for the commencement ceremonies." When she heard it was only two hours, she asked if she could come and meet Vi, my partner. We invited them both for dinner. Since my partner is a clown and children's entertainer, we all ended up blowing up balloons and laughing. They both told us they had begun to be open in their classes about teaching tolerance and dealing with "faggot" jokes and names. Sue was able to be a healing force within her family and within her school, and by her example, to open dialogue where it never happened before.

Every time I teach, I face a room full of strangers and wonder who they are. Given how polarized politics are these days, I feel more careful than in the past. But last month in a group of mostly Mormons in Salt Lake City, I introduced myself as someone with a partner named Vi. And, like in some other classes, one person found the courage to "come out" to me as gay. And maybe the Mormon students breathed a little easier because they could be more transparent about who they were.

My colleagues and I at Lesley have struggled over the years when teaching in the Bible Belt South, dealing with overt racism and with black and white students who feared, even hated, our liberal social ideas. And as I struggled with how to address the racism among the students, they probably struggled with how to fit me, whom they liked, into their categories. I made it okay for me to be who I am, and it also became okay for them to write poems about loving Jesus. The only thing I asked was that they use fresh words, their own words, instead of what they had heard from some preacher. I wanted to hear about their own experiences of Jesus.

Poems demand emotional honesty, and to write powerfully, we must all step out of whatever closet we're in. One student in San Diego recently wrote a poem beginning with the prompt, "I used to..., but now...," and stumbled upon her own aging. She was probably the oldest student in the class, in her early sixties, but her poem took her to places she had tried hard to ignore—her body was changing, there was a limit to her time on earth, she had feelings she had denied about aging. By working this out in the writing of one poem, she was able to shed a few tears, confess her fear to the class through her poem, and applaud herself in the process. We're all coming out in one way or another.

Troubling the Coming-Out Discourse: *The (Non) Outing of My Buzz Cut*

Anne Stebbins

❧

The first few years of my high-school teaching career were turbulent, disastrous, and exhilarating. I was one of the lucky few in my cohort to secure a job immediately upon graduation, and I began my teaching career not unlike many new grads: blissfully unprepared and irresponsibly hopeful. During that time in my muddy young life I was also toying with the idea of *being* lesbian. I was itching to meet gay women but I had no idea where to find them in the conservative city where I lived and worked. One cold January night I attended a formal event with a friend. After an hour of failed attempts at hailing a cab home my date and I stumbled into the local gay bar. I was well liquored and wearing a sparkly ball gown. He drank a beer awkwardly at the bar; I slid onto the dance floor and danced my frost bitten toes back to life in the arms of a beautiful woman. That night I met my first girlfriend and lost myself in her glossy black hair.

Unfortunately our same-sex relationship complicated my teaching identity. I felt that the queer direction of my desire was unintelligible to my school community. I felt incredibly constrained. Yet, my status as a new teacher also contributed to my sense of vulnerability; I thought that if my sexual orientation was discovered it would be detrimental to my teaching career. I felt desperate to protect myself from the homophobic consequences I imagined would ensue if my queer sexuality was known. I imagined my queerness as the centre of myself, as something that I could shut off when I taught. There were numerous strategies that I employed to accomplish this. For example, I repeatedly found myself in tight spaces and conversations where I told (mis) information about myself in order to guard my dangerous secret. Was I single? Yes. Would I like to be set up with a colleague's son? Yes. The incessant lies started to close in on me. Desperate to protect myself, I became obsessed with my appearance. I selected outfits with precision and care and agonized over every tiny detail. I adorned myself with earrings, necklaces, skirts, and high-heals. It was an admittedly crass attempt at feminizing my already femme body. All too soon I was worn out by the effort.

My exhaustion motivated me to contemplate the possibility of "coming-out" as a way of liberating myself from my predicament. I imagined myself announcing my sexual preference by making a declarative statement to the staff and students at my school. I approached my sexuality as a one-dimensional object that could be outed because I believed that the telling of my secret would allow me to move more easily in the space that I inhabited with my students. I believed that 'coming-out' would relieve the tension I felt between my sexuality and my teaching identity. I rehearsed my outing speech in front of the mirror at home and I began advocating on behalf of queer issues at school. I invited a guest speaker from the AIDS Society to speak to my English class, agreed to be the teacher representative for the school's Gay Straight Alliance Club and attended a homophobia themed workshop held by the board. Challenging some of the heteronormative nonsense at school relieved some of my stress but I continued to feel anxious about the possibility of spelling out the secret of my sexual identity.

As I advocated on behalf of queer issues I continued to encounter resistance from the school community. My request that a transgender student be permitted to use the gender neutral staff bathroom was denied by an administrator who declared that the student would just have to "choose" a gender and select a bathroom accordingly. The Gay Straight Alliance's interest in holding a movie night was denied by an administrator who was worried that parent council was not ready for "that kind of event" to be endorsed by the school. The black marker inscriptions "FAG" violently sprawled across several lockers and bathroom doors remained even after my continued appeals to have them removed. I felt worn down and trapped by the homophobic school culture.

After spring break I returned to school sporting a fresh crew cut. During the holiday week I realized that I wanted to shave off my shoulder length blond hair. My return to school initially felt like a triumphant exodus; I considered my hair cut to be a lavish way of performing my queerness that I could take delight in! I felt that my hair cut made me visible as lesbian, and I returned from spring break eager to wear my queerness. However, the staff and students at school eagerly adopted the narrative that I donated my hair to charity. It was easier for me to be the gracious teacher who donated her hair then the unruly dyke who buzzed her head. Instead of transgressing the boundaries of what I believed to be the acceptable female teaching appearance, I became a gracious heroine. The knowledge that the school community had of me enabled them to encounter my buzz cut and anti-homophobic politics without assigning me as queer. Perhaps my slender body and pretty face enabled me to easily pass as a "straight-enough" woman. Regardless of the inaccurate account circulating about my haircut I felt liberated walking around school comfortably in my own skin.

After shaving off my hair, I began to call into question the necessity that I previously felt about coming-out. The non-queer reaction of the school community to my hair cut made me realize that coming-out did not offer any sort of guarantees. I wondered: what was really behind my desire to be out at school? If I was striving to offer myself as a queer-positive representative to students then I had certainly failed in this endeavour. Was I simply looking for recognition? Did I want to disrupt the uncomplicated version of heterosexuality that permeated the school? Was I positioning young queer students as victims who I could rescue by coming-out in the homophobic school environment? The act of shaving my head opened up many questions for me about what it meant to be a queer teacher.

While I had previously longed to announce my sexuality to my students, I began to understand that making this type of declarative statement would not necessarily have released me from the contradictions and difficulties that I faced as a lesbian teacher. In fact, this decision would have forced me to deliberately fashion how I presented my queerness to my students. Would my feminine, white body have unsettled my students or would my queerness have presented itself as safe and unthreatening? Far from liberating me from my quandary, a deliberate statement describing my sexual preference would have presented many questions and dilemmas. In short, naming my sexuality at school would not necessarily have spelled out my queerness in a way that was uncomplicated or even intelligible. On the other hand, by refusing to name a queer sexuality I continued to teach in a tight space where others perceived me to be a heterosexual woman. I moved away from positioning my outing as a solution and started exploring the pedagogical possibilities of my queerness.

Educational research hailing itself as queer theory often invites sexual minority teachers to tell their stories. This telling is usually framed within the distinction of the coming-out narrative which, not surprisingly, is also a feature of my story. The metaphorical teaching closet of educational research continues to draw a clean distinction between teachers who are in and out. My experience as a classroom teacher enables me to sympathize with the coming-out story but lately I am curious about what it might mean to move beyond it. I am concerned that the coming-out narrative continues to position sexuality as a secret of the self that has the potential to reveal the entirety of a person. When I was teaching high-school I felt like my sexuality was located at the center of myself and if the truth about my sexual preference were known my life as a teacher could simply unravel. My sexuality was dangerous; it was something concrete that held me together but it could also undo me. The exposure of my secret self offered the allusion of finality which was called into question after I shaved my head.

I no longer regard my sexuality as a source of truth about myself. Instead of understanding my sexual orientation as a static identity I am currently thinking about queerness as a site of imagined possibilities. Particularly, I understand sexuality as a source of pedagogical possibility that is present in my encounters with teaching and learning. What comes into focus when I look outside binary discourses such as hetero/homo and in/out, is that teaching and learning are incredibly complicated activities. There is a curiosity about the way that I constitute and repudiate my sexual identity that gives me room to allow my sexuality to move. For example, I feel like I am being more generous with myself and my students by marking space in my literature classroom to approaching sexuality as a question instead of exploring it as a certainty. When I encounter an unfamiliar or unruly sexuality in a text I try to resist my urge to contain or label it. As my students and I learn to tolerate uncertainty and ambivalence we also learn to explore ideas together in ways that allow us to open up our ideas about sexuality and consider our own implications in the structures that make sexuality intelligible. My sexual orientation no longer feels like a terrible secret that is concealed and punctuated by my body. I do not locate my sexuality at the center of myself; it lies both within and outside of my body as I playfully take it up in the indeterminate space of teaching.

The Two-Step
Holly St. Jean

❧

Teaching is a lot like dancing; at least it is for me. And, although I am a professional teacher, I am not a professional dancer. It makes no difference that I may dance like Elaine Bennes on Seinfeld, in my mind I move like Ginger Rogers. Metaphorically, of course, I dance everyday in the classroom. We all do, teachers, I mean. Good ones anyway. In order to present our subject matter in meaningful ways, we develop rhythms and styles, organically our own, yet influenced by traditional mainstays. Phys Ed. instructors line dance; science and math educators hip-hop; foreign language pros do a pg-rated tango, art and music types combine ballet, modern, and jazz, and those who teach history and literature try to waltz. As an English teacher, who just happens to be a lesbian, I find myself doing the two-step.

Traditionally, the two-step is a ballroom dance in 2/4 time that uses long, sliding steps. My two-step changes accordingly with every new batch of students, parents, and administrators; my sliding steps vary in length with every year's social mores and situations. The ability to adapt is critical; the trick is to remain mindful to the integrity of the dance.

A late bloomer to most things, I started teaching high school at twenty-six, and only *came out*, to myself, my husband, my family and friends, at thirty-two. In June of '97, during a whirlwind of changes - dealing with my *truth*, my divorce, and my new apartment - I realized my two-step in the classroom would change too. No longer a Mrs. but a Ms, and a gay Ms at that, new choreography would be necessary.

My freshman of '97 knew nothing of my personal life. I would remain Mrs. *So-in-so* until the last day of school. I planned to continue two-stepping through my classes and have my nervous breakdown during the summer. Then, I read Julie's journal entry.

It was a Friday. The kids were working in small groups on an assignment related to the novel—*To Kill a Mockingbird*. It was the last class of the day, and I had promised to read and grade their weekly journals, handing them back before the bell. I'd whipped through a dozen or so, before scanning Julie's. Hers was typical—hair styles, music, friends, the mall. I was about to scratch a check-plus on it, until I read the last paragraph. She'd switched from black ink to blue. Why?

"Mrs. *So-in-so*," it read, "I need to ask you a question."

Julie explained that her parents were getting divorced. Her father had met someone. He'd left. Julie had heard her mother use the word "faggot" while crying on the telephone when she thought Julie wasn't around. Later, when she'd stopped crying, her mother told Julie that her father had left them to go live with a friend, a man. Julie's big question to me appeared on the page on its own separate line. *"Even though my father is gay, is it still okay to love him?"*

In mid-twirl, I collapsed on the dance floor. My breakdown started at that moment. Julie's question carried an extra wallop, because my father had done this very same thing. He'd left our family during the summer of '78, and moved to Boston with a friend. (My younger sister and I had thought the friend was a woman.) He'd asked my mother for a divorce. She refused. She was a strict Catholic and obviously in love. She was at a complete loss as to what to do. Who could blame her? My father returned a year later, went through marriage counseling, and returned to "normal." They played their roles as happily married until Dad died in the *oncology ward* at U-Mass Medical Center – of AIDS – September, 1989. (His was one of the first reported cases in Massachusetts.) His obituary stated that he had "succumbed to cancer." My mother said little, even though my sister and I informed her that we'd seen the word "homosexual" on his medical chart. The extended family was silent.

My father had died, so I never had to ask a question like Julie's, although I had wondered what I might have asked him had I known his truth, had he lived.

"Even though my father is gay, is it still okay to love him?"

Knowing it was risky, but I picked up my red pen and in the margin of her entry wrote: "Julie, *of course* you can still love him. He's your dad. He always will be your dad. And, I'm certain that he loves you and always will."

Then I stood and apologized to the kids for completing only half the journals. While passing back those I had corrected, my body betrayed my resolve and tears came. A few kids noticed. Julie noticed. The bell rang.

"Boy, Mrs. *So-in-so* really feels awful about not getting everyone's journal done," I heard a voice say. The students left.

I shut my door, returned to my desk, and wept.

Might *my people*, my friends and family members, be asking themselves - *Could they still love me? Were they allowed to?*

Well, it turned out that they could and they do, and for that I am grateful. Heck, two of *my people* claimed to have known I was a lesbian (now, I'm not sure if these folks are *that* intuitive, but I love them just the same).

In any event, my journey as a gay Ms. in the classroom began with Julie's question. I've thought of Julie and her parents through the years. I wonder how things are today. I like to imagine Julie's father, a man slightly older than me, oh say fifty-ish, and his handsome partner welcoming Julie into their home at Thanksgiving. Julie is twenty-seven and finishing her residency at a major medical center. Following the meal, just as coffee is being served, Julie's mother and husband arrive. They are between relatives' homes and have popped in for a short visit. Julie's mother unloads her famous pumpkin pie. Everyone smiles and eats.

This is my wish for Julie. However, being that I am not totally delusional, I understand that her family may be nothing like this. Things may have turned out drastically different, which leads me to another student—Andrea.

Andrea was a student in my sophomore lit. course in 2001. By this time, my life had begun. I felt good. Finally, I understood that that *extra-special-more-than-a-friend-ache* I sometimes had for certain girlfriends since age eleven, was simply who I was. And that the only thing that was a "choice" about the whole matter was my making a conscious decision to hide no longer. With help from my therapist, and friends who began introducing me to their gay siblings, I found a local community. I met my very first lesbians. I fit in.

Because I was happy, my two-step in the classroom was dazzling. I was bursting with new ideas and perspectives. I won a tri-community teaching award, and in 2000 I'd actually been *recruited* for a teaching position at a larger regional high school in the next district. The pay was much better. I bought a house; I fell in love. And, get this – I'd fallen in love with a teacher, a woman who worked for a school district in the city.

Things seemed never better. My dance was freer because this school, I discovered the day of my interview, had a GSA (Gay Straight Alliance). I'd never heard of such an organization. Students actually attended and ran this weekly club and an advisor actually advised. Gay and straight students discussed world-wide issues related to sexuality. They went on field trips to other high schools and met with other GSAs. They talked about equality. I'd sat in on a couple of the meetings and each time I felt like pirouetting in the parking lot. What a compassionate and enlightened school system had I the honor of working for. What a wonderful corner of the planet. I considered placing my favorite framed photo of my love and me on my desk, the one of us in the yard with our German shepherd puppy between us.

Then, Andrea.

In December, I decided to have the students read Oscar Wilde's short story, *The Happy Prince.* If you haven't read it, the Happy Prince is a beautiful tale of friendship, love, and sacrifice. It is a good story. I usually have the students write about the meaning and draw their favorite scenes, captioned by favorite lines (Wilde uses dynamite imagery and description that allow for vivid student artwork). This is a lesson that usually engages every class. Usually. I still teach this story today, yet I tend to hold my breath, ever cautious of another student reaction like Andrea's.

Andrea was a mediocre student, content with a D. She had long blonde hair and light blue eyes. She was pretty, but a rough and tumble tom-boy who wore ripped T-shirts, and work boots. Her friends were boys who were also the friends of her older brothers. She had an impressive knowledge of dirt bikes and sports cars. I never had any problem with her in class. In fact, because she was different, I found her intriguing. During class, she was quiet and polite, until *The Happy Prince.*

As I distributed the story, I explained that its author was a man named Oscar Wilde. The hand of the shining A student in the class, a boy whose name I can't recall, asked, "Didn't Oscar Wilde write a book called *The Picture of Dorian Gray?*"

"Yes," I replied.

"Thought so," he said. "I read that."

"Great," I said.

"Hey, did you know that Oscar Wilde was gay?"

Before I could respond with a yes, Andrea stood up, threw her books and story to the floor and announced, "I'm not reading any fucking story by a fucking faggot!" Following this pronouncement, she stormed out of the room.

Up until this point, there were few adjustments I'd had to make to my two-step in regards to anything dealing with homosexuality. Correcting language was one—when students said—*That's so gay!*— I'd tell them not to say it, and when they called one another *gay*, I'd tell them to be kind. Clarifying language was another adjustment— when we read *Catcher in the Rye*, we thoughtfully discussed Holden's references to "flits, lesbians, and poofs," and his confusion as to the intentions of his former teacher—Mr. Antolini.

So, what shocked me about Andrea's outburst to some degree was the fact that we'd already studied readings and had limited discussions these sorts of issues. What frightened me about her outburst was the unexpected violence—the profanity, the book slamming, the door slamming, and the fact that she'd run away.

All eyes were on me, of course, to view my next move. Oddly enough, not one student uttered a comment or made that annoying "Ooooh!" sound that traditionally accompanies bad behavior. Like me, they were stunned.

I phoned the assistant principal. I explained that Andrea had sworn in class and run out. He told me write a disciplinary slip. He told me that he'd find her and deal with her. I thanked him and hung up. What I did next surprised me. I took a breath, looked at the student who had asked about Wilde, and started dancing, "Yes. Oscar Wilde was gay. In fact, he was imprisoned because he was gay. Now, let's read the story."

Andrea's punishment was minimal. She received a stern talking to by the assistant principal, a day's internal suspension, and she was required to write an apology for insubordination. She read her apology to me in the presence of the assistant principal. They'd come to my room minutes after the last bell. Red-faced and trembling (due to humiliation and anger) she read: "I'm sorry I said what I said. I didn't mean to upset you or the class. I didn't mean to disrupt the class."

Then, she lowered the paper, stared right at me, and said, "Look, I'm sorry, but it's just the way I've been raised. Ask anyone in my family and you'll get the same reaction."

The assistant principal glancing at me from the doorway, raised an eyebrow, and gave a sad nod, "Okay, Andrea," he said, "That's enough. Let's go."

That was it.

After Andrea, I decided to get more involved. Like several other teachers, I allowed the GSA students to place a pink triangle sticker on my classroom door. I participated in the annual Day of Silence and I asked to chaperone the annual field trip to North Hampton, Massachusetts for the GLBT Leadership Conference. If my students weren't catching on that I was gay, my colleagues definitely were, especially since my partner had been hired in 2002 and everyone noticed that we carpooled daily. The atmosphere remained polite, no one asked any questions. My partner and I didn't tell.

In 2005, the sort of trouble my mother had cautioned me about when I came out—*mean people*—happened. The GSA students gained permission from the principal to show the 2002 HBO movie adaptation of Moses Kaufman's play—*The Laramie Project*—as part of Diversity Week, a week filled with student activities relating to anti-discrimination. The film is concerned with the 1998 hate crime against Matthew Shepard, a gay college student, murdered in Laramie, Wyoming. The film, in an edited, 45 minute format, was shown to the entire student body. The next morning, newspaper and television reporters swarmed the school to interview the principal, the GSA advisor, teachers, and students. The press had been contacted by concerned parents angered that no prior notification had been given about the school-wide assembly. Some parents argued that they should have received an "Opt-Out" waiver to sign ensuring that their children not see the film.

Evident in every written and aired report was the reality that some parents feared indoctrination. And as it turned out, one of these parents was a very vocal school committee member, and one was the wife of a prominent teacher.

In an article dated Wednesday, May 18, 2005, the principal said, "I don't think we were promoting homosexuality. I think we were promoting tolerance."

In the same article, the school committee member, a community businessman, paraphrased the wife of the prominent teacher, saying he agreed with her view that, "It's not the school's job to teach morals and ethics."

For the first time my two-step became a frantic Russian folk dance involving strong crossed arms and a lot of leaping and kicking. I wrote an editorial. It was published in the Worcester Telegram and Gazette. In it, I praised the student editor of the high school paper who wrote that the film taught students the danger of hate crimes and the importance of tolerance. Then, I told both *Mr. School- Committee and Mrs. Teacher's-Wife* that, "morals and ethics are interwoven in curriculum." And, I asked them if they really thought that, "literature could be taught without asking students to analyze the moral dilemmas characters face?" I concluded with, "Challenging students to consider what is controversial helps prepare them for the real world, a place filled with diversity. Teaching morals and ethics is my job."

My editorial caused debate. Some critics admired my interpretive dance, some did not. Mrs. *Teacher's-Wife* wrote a three page letter and sent it to my home. She insisted that after viewing the film, her son had been "angered" that the film portrayed anyone disagreeing with the "homosexual lifestyle was shown as hateful and unintelligent." She argued that her son should not have been "exposed" to the film without her permission as one of her family's core beliefs is that "the homosexual lifestyle is not an acceptable alternative." She ended her letter with, "Do you have children, Ms. *So-in so*? (Clearly, her husband informed her that I didn't.) Wouldn't you want that right?"

What I find amazing is that many people with children assume that the childless cannot possibly fathom the enormous responsibility connected with child-rearing. They believe that *they-who-have-spawn*, (and usually not those who have adopted or who have been inseminated – but only those who have bred through traditional means) have been endowed with a mystical wisdom. (My partner says I am too sensitive about this issue. She says I should lighten up.) But, darn it! *They-who-have-not-spawn* can understand children.

Another assumption in society that I find incredible is that some people believe that gays are not religious. In 2007, a colleague I'd co-taught with for three years learned that I'd agreed to be the GSA advisor for one semester while the current advisor (a very straight woman) took maternity leave. This colleague was the first to ask me if I were a lesbian. When I confirmed, she said, "I'm so sorry, but because of my religious beliefs concerning *your lifestyle*, I cannot work with you anymore."

When I consider it now, I guess I did suspect her unease when facing that pink triangle on my door everyday, but I never saw this coming. This woman had effectively halted my dance steps, as if she'd taken my legs out from under me with the handle of a broom or a billy club.

However, as she stood before me unwavering and tethered to her piety, I got back on my feet and felt a positive cosmic force bolstering me. "You know, people with *my lifestyle* believe in God, too. And, I'm pretty sure He loves me as much as He loves you," I said.

She gave me a strange smile dripping with pity and walked out. She was reassigned to someone else's class. I was never approached by her supervisor or any administrator about her decision.

I continued dancing.

I'm still dancing. And as the years progress, my two-step gets easier. Despite the occasional challenge from those *who-are-who-they-are* and will not or cannot change, there are more frequent rewards from twice as many who have adapted, who can tolerate and who do understand. My partner and I have many colleagues we consider great friends. We have met sensitive and supportive parents. And, we agree that most of our students are aware and accepting.

In 2008, a new principal asked the GSA advisor, the health teacher, and me to assist with a Professional Development Day. This particular day's theme was Diversity. A new set of Massachusetts standards mandated training for Massachusetts teachers. Prejudice and bullying issues were central.

The day took some clever dance moves from all of us. One of my students, Dan, an openly gay senior volunteered to address the entire faculty. Dan described his life as a gay teen, including the fact that he lived with is grandparents, because his parents had told him to leave. Overall, Dan's speech was positive and inspiring. He influenced minds. His dancing was phenomenal.

This year, at teacher-parent conferences, I met Karen's two moms, her biological dad and her step-mom (talk about parental support), and I met Joe's two dads, a fifty-ish couple who had just adopted him from the foster care system. Karen and Joe's parents (the entire gang) thanked me for provided their kids with such a comfortable, non-threatening classroom environment. I was honored.

As part of a Community Service Learning Project, I required students in my AP Composition class to write memoir pieces. Joe wrote about his adoption. He shared it in class and gained cheers and applause. He seemed thrilled. Only, when it came time to actually place his memoir in the class collection, Joe was hesitant. He knew that the superintendent and principal would receive copies and that booklets would be on display in the school library and in all five town libraries. I asked Joe to go home and talk it over with his parents. Then, before

Joe left class, I called him to my desk. "Joe," I said, staring at him with my most intense teacher gaze, "you realize that I have a lot in common with your dads, don't you? If you were my son, I'd definitely want you to include your work."

Joe was a bit confused, so I used my best dancer's exaggerated arm sweep and pointed to that darn triangle on my door.

"Ohhh!" Joe said, "Really?"

The following morning, Joe dropped off his memoir before classes began. He wore a huge smile. "My dads agreed. Please put my memoir in with the rest."

So, what is it like being a high school teacher who happens to be a lesbian? It is a wonder-filled dance recital, just as I'm sure it is for every dedicated teacher. It's a two-step.

CONTRIBUTORS

ↂ

Laura M. André holds a Ph.D. in art history from the University of North Carolina at Chapel Hill. After a stint as a university professor, she now works as a consultant for a major independent bookseller specializing in rare and contemporary photography books. Her writing has been published in *Ask Me About My Divorce: Women Open Up About Moving On*, and in *Mothering* magazine. She recently co-edited (with Candace Walsh) *Dear John, I Love Jane: Women Write About Leaving Men for Women*, a Seal Press anthology released in 2010. She lives in Santa Fe, New Mexico.

Anne Balay is an Assistant Professor of English at Indiana University Northwest, where she teaches American literature, Children's Literature, and Gender Studies. She has published articles on Kathleen Norris, female masculinities in children's fiction, Gene Stratton-Porter, and queer fantasy fiction for young adults.

Lissa Brown is a former high school history teacher who enjoyed a second, award-winning public relations and marketing career. She's been a columnist, speechwriter and ghostwriter for public and business officials. Writing as Leslie Brunetsky, she is the author of *Real Country: From the Fast Track to Appalachia*, named Humor Book of the Year (2009) by the NC High Country Writers. Lissa offers workshops on writing humor and media relations. She may be contacted at LJBMAU@skybest.com.

Sarah B. Burghauser is an LA-based writer, scholar, and mixed-media artist. She holds an MFA in Writing from Cal-Arts, an MA from Oregon State, and has published in *A Café in Space*, the Anaïs Nin literary journal. Her creative and scholarly fields of expertise include feminist studies, queer culture, erotic literature, and intersections of religion and sexuality. Sarah is a 2010 Fellow of the Lambda Literary Writer's Retreat and has read her work at the L.A. Queer Studies Conference, Skylight Books, Redcat and other venues. Currently, Sarah looks forward to her residency at The MacDowell Colony, where she will work on her first book, *Nincarnation*, a text, which insists it is possible to know oneself in the life of another.

Barbara DiBernard is a professor of English and Women's & Gender Studies at the University of Nebraska-Lincoln, where she has taught since 1978. She teaches courses in women's literature, 20th/21st Century Lesbian Literature, and LGBT Studies and incorporates disability studies into all of her courses. Currently she is co-teaching a new course on Gender and the Global Politics of Food. She has been director of Women's Studies and was one of the founders of the LGBTQ/Sexuality Studies minor. She lives happily in Lincoln, NE with her partner of 22 years, and in her free time swims, gardens, walks, and goes bird watching.

B.J. Epstein is a lecturer in literature and translation at the University of East Anglia in Norwich, England. She is also a writer, editor, and translator from Swedish to English. She can be reached via her website http://www.awaywithwords.se or her blog on translation http://brave-new-words.blogspot.com/.

With roots stretching from rural Nebraska, **Stacy Fox** has truly found home in Chicago. As a high school English teacher on the South Side, Stacy has worked to implement slam poetry and finger painting into her classroom as a way of tricking her students into learning. She writes lesson plans to trick administrators into thinking that her students are getting more out of her work with them than she is. She loves her fiancé and refuses to let some pesky little marriage legislation get in the way of her right to smash wedding cake into the facial pores of the woman she loves.

Jessica Gardner is a twenty-four year old, openly gay female who currently lives in Brooklyn, New York. She grew up in Southern California and attended Stanford University, where she double-majored in International Relations and Anthropological Sciences. She moved to New York City after graduating in 2008, to begin time with Teach for America. For the past two years she has taught middle school special education in the Bronx while completing a Masters in Education from City College. She intends to continue teaching for as long as she can successfully dodge pencils.

Carol Guess is the author of six books of poetry and prose, including *Switch* and *Tinderbox Lawn*. A new collection of prose poems, *Doll Studies: Forensics*, will be published by Black Lawrence Press in 2012. She is an Associate Professor of English at Western Washington University, where she teaches Queer Studies and Creative Writing.

Lori Horvitz is the editor of this anthology. Her short stories, poetry, and personal essays have appeared in a variety of literary journals and anthologies including *The Southeast Review, Hotel Amerika, Thirteenth Moon, Dos Passos Review, Quarter After Eight* and *P.S.: What I Didn't Say: Unsent Letters to Our Female Friends* (Seal Press). A native New Yorker, Lori now makes her home in North Carolina, where she is an Associate Professor of Literature and Language at UNC-Asheville.

A native of Philadelphia, **Mara Conroy Hughes** received her bachelor's degree from Sarah Lawrence College. One of roughly 6,000 New Jersey teachers laid off as a result of Republican governor Chris Christie's $900 million cuts to education, she is now pursuing graduate study at Rutgers University in Sociology of Education. This is her first published essay.

Sassafras Lowrey is an internationally award-winning storyteller, author, artist, and educator. She believes that everyone has a story to tell and that the telling of stories is essential in the creation of social change. Sassafras is the editor of the *Kicked Out Anthology* (Homofactus Press, 2010), which brings together the voices of current and former homeless LGBTQ youth, and her prose has been included in numerous anthologies. Sassafras regularly teaches LGBTQ storytelling workshops at colleges and conferences across the country. To learn more about Sassafras and her work, visit www. PoMoFreakshow.com and www.KickedOutAnthology.com.

Liz Matelski is a Ph.D. candidate at Loyola University Chicago in 19th and 20th century American history. Her academic work focuses on body image, sexuality, and popular culture. She is currently finishing her dissertation, "The Color(s) of Perfection: The Feminine Body, Beauty Ideals, and Identity in Postwar America, 1945–1970" which studies American women's body image in the white, black, and lesbian communities.

Bonnie Morris is an out lesbian professor and the author of eight books, including three Lambda Literary Award finalists. Her most recent book is *Revenge of the Women's Studies Professor,* an entire volume on how homophobia drives the backlash against students and professors of women's history. In Washington D.C., she is on the board of Mothertongue, a spoken-word stag for local women, and her essays and stories have appeared in over sixty anthologies of lesbian and feminist writing.

Jules Odendahl-James is currently a Lecturing Fellow at Duke University. Her research focuses on intersections of truth, memory, and activism in forensic and documentary media. A founding member of Bold Maids Feminist Performance Company (1996–2003), she has fashioned multiple performance scripts critical of pedagogy, cultural theory, and popular culture with collaborators Marla Morton and Kelly Rowett-James. Their pieces include *The Three Faces of Ophelia, or What's a Nice Girl Like You Doing in a River Like This?, Queerer than Thou: The Game Show that Everyone Can Play, Inauguration Gay,* and *Fetus or We'll Starve: A Rhapsody on Feminist Parenting.*

Mary Clare Powell is a professor at Lesley University, formerly Director of the Creative Arts in Learning Division, who teaches poetry to teachers across the country. She has published several books, including *This Way Daybreak Comes: Women's Values and the Future, The Widow, Arts, Education and Social Change* (editor). She is the author of several books of poetry, including *Things Owls Ate, Academic Scat,* and *In the Living Room.* She lives in Greenfield, Massachusetts where she works on the Franklin County Arts and Culture Partnership, and is on the Board of Trustees of the Pioneer Valley Performing Arts Charter School in South Hadley. She writes articles on integrated arts in education and poetry.

Lee Ann Roripaugh is the author of three volumes of poetry: *Beyond Heart Mountain* (Penguin, 1999), *Year of the Snake* (Southern Illinois

University Press, 2004), and *On the Cusp of a Dangerous Year* (Southern Illinois University Press, 2009). She is a Professor of English at The University of South Dakota, where she teaches creative writing and multicultural literature.

Maureen Seaton has authored twelve poetry collections. Her latest is *Cave of the Yellow Volkswagen* (Carnegie Mellon, 2009). Her memoir, *Sex Talks to Girls* (University of Wisconsin, 2008), won the Lambda Literary Award. Previous collections have won the Audre Lorde Award, the Iowa Poetry Prize, and the Lambda Literary Award. In 2011 two books are due: *Stealth* (Chax Press) with Samuel Ace; and *Sinéad O'Connor and Her Coat of a Thousand Bluebirds* (Sentence Book Award), with Neil de la Flor. The recipient of an NEA and the Pushcart, Seaton teaches poetry at the University of Miami.

Jennifer Smith is a young writer living in Melbourne. She has too much education and not enough furniture. She recently completed her English Honours in creative writing at La Trobe University and can prod protagonists and antagonists about the page well enough. She is best described as a small, oddly adjusted person with a lot of stories in her head and a mild obsession with avocados.

Kristie Soares is a Ph.D. student in Comparative Literature at the University of California, Santa Barbara. Her article "From Canary Birds to Suffrage: Lavinia's Feminist Role in *Who Would Have Thought It?*" was recently published in *Letras Femeninas*. Soares also served as guest editor for the Latin American issue of academic review journal, *Counterpoise Magazine*. Her research interests include Queer U.S. Latina/o Literature, Contemporary Cuban-American literature, 20th Century Brazilian Poetry, Gender Politics, and Performance Art.

Michelle Spiegel is a graduate student working on her Master's Degree in Women's, Gender and Sexuality Studies at The Ohio State University and will soon be pursuing a Ph.D. in Multicultural and Equity Studies in Education. Michelle teaches an undergraduate course at the University entitled *Gender, Sex and Power*. Her research interests address issues of sexuality and education. Current projects include a piece that interrogates problematic queer representations in children's literature that are monolithic, homonormative, and teach "tolerance" and one that contemplates how educators can use cyber technologies to encourage queer students' navigation of multiple (sexual) subjectivities and feel validated in the heteronormative space of the classroom.

Anne Stebbins is a Ph.D. student at the Faculty of Education at York University in Toronto, Ontario. She received her undergraduate and graduate degrees from the University of Western Ontario in London, Ontario, where she also taught high school. Her current scholarship focuses on queer, female, secondary school teachers and their embodied experiences of teaching and learning.

Holly St. Jean is proud to be a resident of Massachusetts. Despite the stoic reputation assigned to New Englanders, she has always found most to be pleasant and fair. Actually, she believes that people–everywhere–could be *pleasant and fair* if only they would make an effort to understand one another. Holly's favorite quote by Marcel Proust is: "The voyage of discovery is not in seeking new landscapes but in having new eyes." She has been a dedicated high school English teacher for twenty years, and remains in a loving and committed relationship with her partner of eleven years.

Cynthia Tyler is the author of two novels, *Descanso* (Haworth Press, 2005), and *Shadow Work* (Haworth Press, 2006). She lives in Pasadena, California with her partner and their two Golden Retrievers, Athena and Kip. Visit her at www.cynthiatyler.com

Shannon Weber is a doctoral student of Feminist Studies at the University of California, Santa Barbara, as well as a proud alumna of the Critical Social Thought program at Mount Holyoke College. Her research interests are LGBTQ politics, identity discourses, popular culture and new media, and the history of same-sex desire and love in the United States. She is currently investigating the historical construction of selected Seven Sisters colleges as queer spaces and how this translates into contemporary queer communities on campus.

Sandy Woodson has taught ethics, environmental philosophy and writing at the Colorado School of Mines since 1999. She earned an M.A. in Environmental Ethics from Colorado State University, and an MFA in Creative Nonfiction from the University of Montana. Woodson received the Associated Writing Program's "Intro Award" for new writers, and has previously been published in *The Cimarron Review* and *The Bellevue Literary Review*. She lives with her wife, Meghan, in Denver, Colorado.

Studies in the Postmodern Theory of Education

General Editor
Shirley R. Steinberg

Counterpoints publishes the most compelling and imaginative books being written in education today. Grounded on the theoretical advances in criticalism, feminism, and postmodernism in the last two decades of the twentieth century, Counterpoints engages the meaning of these innovations in various forms of educational expression. Committed to the proposition that theoretical literature should be accessible to a variety of audiences, the series insists that its authors avoid esoteric and jargonistic languages that transform educational scholarship into an elite discourse for the initiated. Scholarly work matters only to the degree it affects consciousness and practice at multiple sites. Counterpoints' editorial policy is based on these principles and the ability of scholars to break new ground, to open new conversations, to go where educators have never gone before.

For additional information about this series or for the submission of manuscripts, please contact:

Shirley R. Steinberg
c/o Peter Lang Publishing, Inc.
29 Broadway, 18th floor
New York, New York 10006

To order other books in this series, please contact our Customer Service Department:

(800) 770-LANG (within the U.S.)
(212) 647-7706 (outside the U.S.)
(212) 647-7707 FAX

Or browse online by series:
www.peterlang.com